Five-Minute Brain Workout

Five-Minute Brain Workout

Games and Puzzles to Keep Your Mind Sharp and Supple

by
Kim Chamberlain

Skyhorse Publishing

Skyhorse Publishing books may be purchased in bulk at special discounts
for sales promotion, corporate gifts, fund-raising, or educational purposes.
Special editions can also be created to specifications. For details, contact the Special Sales Department, Skyhorse Publishing, 307 West 36th
Street, 11th Floor, New York, NY 10018 or info@skyhorsepublishing.com.

Skyhorse® and Skyhorse Publishing® are registered trademarks of Skyhorse Publishing, Inc.®, a Delaware corporation.

Visit our website at www.skyhorsepublishing.com.

10 9 8 7 6 5 4 3 2 1

Library of Congress Cataloging-in-Publication Data is available on file.

ISBN: 978-1-62636-019-8

Printed in the United States of America

Contents

Introduction

Hello and welcome!

This is a brain training book based on word games and puzzles.

Taking care of your brain can be equally as useful as taking care of your body. Regularly doing a series of short, varied tasks can keep your mind sharp and flexible. The key to stimulating your brain is to constantly learn, and to regularly challenge your brain with new tasks.

Research shows that brain training games help improve your memory, concentration, problem-solving skills, processing speed, creativity, logic and reasoning.

We learn more if three factors are present: if we are doing something we enjoy; if there is repetition; if there is variety. For these reasons the book uses a games and puzzles theme aimed at people who enjoy words and language; there are ten examples of the same kind of game or puzzle; and there is a wide variety of types of games and puzzles.

By doing both games and puzzles it will give you the **discipline** that comes with finding the 'correct' answer required for puzzles, along with the **creativity** of a range of acceptable answers that a game provides.

You have enough for a year's worth of working your brain, so feel free to get started . . . and enjoy!

How the book is laid out

Games & Puzzles
There are 365 exercises—enough for one a day—comprising 37 different types of word games and puzzles, spaced evenly throughout the book. 36 types have ten exercises, while the 37th has five exercises.

Levels
There are ten levels, Level 1 through to Level 10, generally increasing in difficulty as you go through the book. This means that the tenth exercise will usually be harder than the ones preceding it.

The difference between a game and a puzzle
Generally speaking a puzzle has a specific answer, for example a Word Search, whereas a game doesn't, and may have a number of suitable answers, for example "Think of 10 adjectives starting with the letter A."
Approximately two thirds of the exercises are puzzles, while the rest are games.

Variety
There is a wide variety of types of exercises (37 to be exact) specifically devised to make your brain work in different ways and keep it alert.

Bonus
Try the bonus puzzles at the end. They are a teaser from the next book!

Answers
You will find the answers at the back of the book. The puzzles have specific answers, while the games have examples of acceptable answers.

How to use this book

First of all, feel free to use the book in any way you like, there is no right or wrong way to use it.

A suggested way is to start at the beginning with Level 1 games and puzzles, and do one a day until you reach Level 10.

As many of the exercises will be new to you, it's a good idea to take time to read the instructions so that you can use the 5 minutes well.

The games and puzzles will probably take you different amounts of time. Some may not take the full 5 minutes, while some are more involved and may take you slightly longer.

While the puzzles have specific answers, the games don't, which means you can continue developing your creativity by doing them more than once and getting different answers.

If you are not sure how to tackle a game or puzzle, look at the answer and work out how it is done, then you'll know how to do the next one.

As well as a way to exercise your brain, the games and puzzles can be used to challenge yourself, or simply to have fun, or you can bring in a competitive element by using a timer or doing them with others.

The exercises can be used in many settings, for example at home; in work; in social settings; in educational settings such as schools; as ice-breakers and energizers in training sessions, and in therapy settings.

Level 1

WORD TRAIL 1

HOW TO PLAY

Find the 5 words listed in the grid starting with the circled letters
Words go horizontally or vertically.

(E)	N	I	N	G	(E)
E	T	G	A	H	L
R	T	R	N	P	E
I	A	E	T	(E)	L
N	(E)	M	(E)	T	I
Y	N	O	B	I	C

EBONY

ELEPHANT

ELICIT

EMERGING

ENTERTAIN

JOINING WORDS 1

HOW TO PLAY

Find a word that completes the first word and begins the second.

The number in brackets indicates the number of letters that are missing.

DOCT	__ __	ANGE	(2)
HEAL	__ __	IN	(2)
NUR	__ __	AT	(2)
PATI	__ __ __	AIL	(3)
MEDI	__ __ __	MLY	(3)
ILLN	__ __ __	ENCE	(3)
HOSP	__ __ __ __	ICS	(4)
MEDI	__ __ __ __	MA	(4)
THERA	__ __ __ __	ON	(4)

PYRAMID WORDS 1

HOW TO PLAY

Fill in the rows with words of your choice, starting with a 1-letter word, through to a 10-letter word.

LETTER CROSS 1

HOW TO PLAY

Cross out the letters that appear twice.

The remaining letters spell the name of a country.

H	N	M	B	Q	F	K	P
G	J	S	G	O	L	I	D
P		Q	I	V	T	C	E
R	T	B	X		U	L	C
Z	E	J	Z	W	A	M	Y
F	K	V	D	X	S	H	U

SPEED WORDS 1

HOW TO PLAY

Choose 10 words that fit the criteria given.

Choose words that are not proper nouns.

Use a different word for each question.

Choose a word that:		
1	Begins with 'F' and has 2 syllables	
2	Includes a double 'E'	
3	Ends in 'ION'	
4	Has 7 letters	
5	Ends in 'X'	
6	Begins with 'SPA'	
7	Has a 'Z' in the body of the word	
8	Rhymes with 'STEAM'	
9	Is an anagram of 'TEAL'	
10	Begins and ends with the same letter	

WORKING IT OUT 1

HOW TO PLAY

Work out what is unusual about this passage.

I saw six cats in our road. Two black, two brown, and two tabby cats.

All cats had long tails and dirty paws.

A dog was watching, as was a man with two kids.

Four cats ran away. Two sat still, watching and waiting.

X WORDS 1

HOW TO PLAY

Place the correct words in the rows in the grid so that both diagonals spell a four-letter word reading from top to bottom.

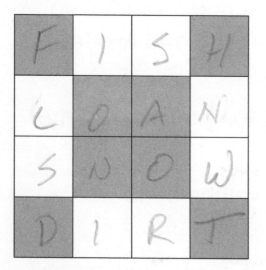

DIRT

SNOW

LOAN

FISH

FDSL
DIRT
LOAN
SNOW
FISH

8

SYNONYMS 1

HOW TO PLAY

Find the ten matching pairs of synonyms in the grid.

Rearrange the four remaining words to form a sentence

HORRIBLE	CARING	ANGRY	SMALL
SOGGY	KEEP	FAST	SLEEPING
TRAINING	BIG	BRAIN	MESSY
UNTIDY	TINY	AWFUL	WEEPING
LOVING	SLUMBERING	YOUR	WET
QUICK	CRYING	LARGE	MAD

Sentence: _KEEP_ _TRAINING_ _YOUR_ _BRAIN_

FIRST AND LAST LETTERS 1

HOW TO PLAY

Think of 10 words where the first and last letters alternate.

For example, if the first word is 'REALLY', the next word would need to start with Y and end with R, the third word would then start with R and end with Y again, and so on.

Example: REALLY – YOUR – RAY – YONDER – RARITY – YEAR – RATIFY – YOUNGER – ROMANY – YOUNGSTER

Using the given words, find another 9 words with alternating first and last letters.

For words ending in S, aim to avoid using plurals.

SHOT	TOSS SOOT TRESSPASS START TREMENDOUS SET TREMULOUS SCOOT TRESS
ENTER	RATE EAGER ROLE ENABLER RITE EMBER RELATE ENTAILER REMOVE
POOL	LAP PAL LOOP BALL CAP PATROL LOOP PILL LIP LOLIPOP PEEL

SPLIT WORDS 1

HOW TO PLAY

There are eight 4-letter words that have been split into 2-letter pieces.

Find the matching parts of the eight words.

Topic: Items of clothing

BO	CA	LT	SO
WN	ST	OT	VE
BE	AT	SH	CK
OE	PE	CO	GO

1. VEST
2. SOCK
3. GOWN
4. COAT
5. PELT
6. SHOE
7. BOOT
8. CABE

MEMORY GRID 1

HOW TO PLAY

Study the grid, and remember the position of the words.

Then turn the page and answer the questions.

Topic: Colors

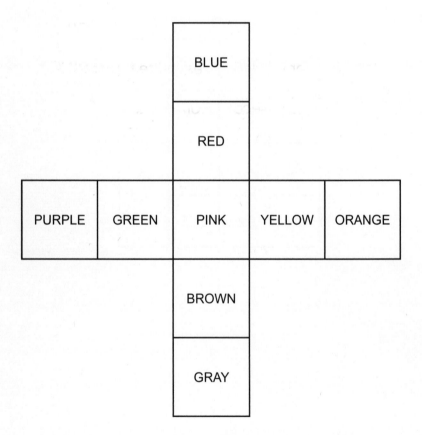

MEMORY GRID 1

Questions

1. Which color is directly above BROWN? *PINK*

2. Which color is immediately to the left of *YELLOW* ORANGE?

3. Which color is three spaces below BLUE? *BROWN*

4. Which color is two spaces to the left of PINK? *PURPLE*

5. Which color is second from the top?
   RED

DEFINITIONS 1

HOW TO PLAY

Choose the correct definition for each word.

Gerbil
- African herb of genus gerbera
- A form of Latin verb
- Mouselike rodent

Jorum
- Large drinking bowl
- Middle Eastern dessert
- Bend in a river

Cos
- A cluster of stars
- Kind of lettuce
- Plant similar to a dahlia

Acanthus
- Unaccompanied choral music
- Lazy
- Herbaceous plant

Pontiff
- Flat bottomed boat
- A bridge
- The pope

Milliner
- A person who makes hats
- A farmer who grows cereal
- A period of 1000 years

Beryl
- Collar or cape on a dress
- Transparent mineral
- Hard white metallic element

Yurt
- Milk-based drink
- Mongolian clothing
- Tent made of skins or felt

Flummery
- A type of hat worn in 19th century England
- A soft jelly or porridge made with flour
- A gust of wind

Syzygy
- An informer who denounces others to the authorities
- A haphazard and random approach
- An almost straight-line configuration of three celestial bodies

14

COLUMN WORDS 1

HOW TO PLAY

Place the words in the correct rows in the grid so that columns 2 and 5 spell out six-letter words.

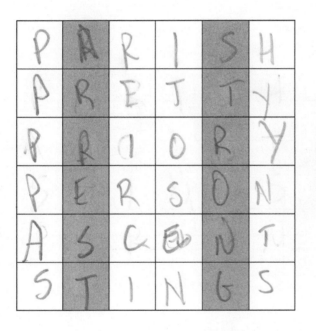

P	A	R	I	S	H
P	R	E	T	T	Y
P	R	I	O	R	Y
P	E	R	S	O	N
A	S	C	E	N	T
S	T	I	N	G	S

PERSON

PARISH

ASCENT

PRIORY

STINGS

PRETTY

EASRTR

TGROSN STRONG

STRINGS 1

HOW TO PLAY

The grid has 30 boxes.

Place words in the boxes, where the last letter of one becomes the first letter of the next. The words must fit exactly into the 30 boxes. Use any words you like

For example:

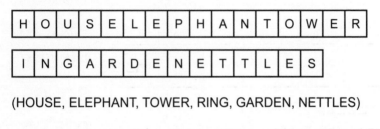

(HOUSE, ELEPHANT, TOWER, RING, GARDEN, NETTLES)

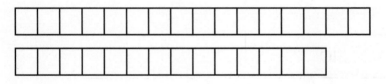

COMBINED ANAGRAMS 1

HOW TO PLAY

Two words have been combined and their letters arranged in alphabetical order.

Can you work out the two words?

For example the words SEVEN and EIGHT would combine to form EEEGHINSTV

Topic: Numbers

	Answer
EEELNTTVW	
EEEILNSVX	
FFFIORTUY	

QUOTE GRID 1

HOW TO PLAY

Included in the grid is a one sentence quote. The words are in a continuous string, and the first word has been circled.

When you have found the quote, put the small letters from each square in the correct order into the empty grid to find a phrase relating to the quote.

O	O		G
SMALL	ONE		MANKIND.
M	**N**	**N**	**N**
THAT'S	STEP	A	FOR
L	**A**	**I**	**D**
FOR	MAN,	LEAP	GIANT

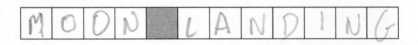

M	O	O	N		L	A	N	D	I	N	G

WORD CAPSULE 1

HOW TO PLAY

Choose six 5-letter words that start with the letter on the left and end with the letters on the right. Choose a different word each time.

For example if the capsule was:

H				C
				L
				O
				U
				D
				Y

Your answers may be:

H	A	V	O	C
	O	V	E	L
	E	L	L	O
	A	I	K	U
	A	T	E	D
	U	R	R	Y

H	O	P	E	S
	E	A	R	T
	A	T	E	R
	O	R	S	E
	O	U	S	E
	A	B	I	T

MISSING ALPHABET 1

HOW TO PLAY

All 26 letters of the alphabet have been removed from this passage.

Can you put them in the correct places?

The alphabet is listed so you can cross off each letter as you place it into the passage

Manuel li_v_ed in an a_p_artment on the si_x_th _f_loor

_S_o he was s_u_rprised to _h_ear the soun_d_ of a ver_y_

la_r_ge an_i_mal _c_oming fr_o_m the ad_j_oining

apart_m_ent.

Ama_z_ed, he couldn'_t_ thin_k_ of a lo_g_ical re_a_son

for this, so _q_uickly _w_ent n_e_xt door to find out. What

a_n_imal cou_l_d it _b_e?

ABCDEFGHIJKLMNOPQRSTUVWXYZ

MINI WORD SUDOKU 1

HOW TO PLAY

Place the letters from the 6-letter word **PENCIL** in the grid so that each column, each row, and each of the six 2×3 sub-grids contains all of the 6 letters from the word.

E	I	C	N	P	L
I	P	E	C	L	N
C	L	I	E	N	P
L	N	P	I	C	E
N	C	L	P	E	I
P	E	N	L	I	C

WORDS FROM A WORD 1

HOW TO PLAY

Choose words that begin with the given letters and fit the category.

For example if the grid contained:

LETTER	CATEGORY	NUMBER OF WORDS
K	Girl's name	1 *KATE*
E	Occupation	2 *ELECTRICIAN ECONOMIST*
N	Place name	3 *NACHES, NAPA, NEVADA*
T	Adjective	4 *THIRSTY, TESTY, TEMPERATE, THIRSTY*

You would need to think of 1 girl's name beginning with K;
2 occupations beginning with; E, 3 place names beginning with N;
4 adjectives beginning with T.

LETTER	CATEGORY	NUMBER OF WORDS	WORDS
K	Animal	1	*KANGAROO*
A	Country	2	*AUSTRALIA, ARGENTINA*
N	Food	3	*NUT, NUTELLA, NOG*
S	Boy's name	4	*SAM, SEAN, STEVE, STEVIE*
A	Girl's name	5	*AMELIA ALICIA, ALEXA, ALICE, ANN*
S	Occupation	6	*STYLIST, SURGEON, SPY, SNOOKER SAMURAI, SKIER, SKATER*

RHYMING WORDS 1

HOW TO PLAY

Find a word that rhymes with the given word and fits the definition.

For example:

WORD	DEFINITION
BARROW	Vegetable

The answer would be
MARROW

WORD	DEFINITION	RHYMING WORD
FABLE	Piece of furniture	TABLE
EIGHT	Dislike	HATE
WEAK	Vegetable	LEEK
FLOWER	Period of time	HOUR
WRITE	Great strength	MIGHT
DONE	Enjoyment	FUN
FIRE	Further up	HIGHER
OWN	Part of a body	BONE
SHOE	Type of tree	YEW
LIST	Failed to hit the mark	MISSED

NAMES 1

HOW TO PLAY

Each row has a five-letter girl's name in it with the letters rearranged, plus one extra letter.

Work out the name, then place the extra letter in the right hand column.

Rearrange the extra letters to make another name.

For example:

						Girl's name	Extra letter
M	A	M	E	S	G	GEMMA	S

						Girl's name	Extra letter
L	Y	L	S	A	N	SALLY	N
N	L	A	N	O	D	DONNA	L
E	L	E	C	N	H	HELEN	C
I	I	L	N	D	A	LINDA	I
A	N	S	S	U	O	SUSAN	O
A	T	A	E	N	I	ANITA	E
Additional name						NICOLE	

REMEMBERING NAMES AND FACES 1

There are various strategies for remembering names and faces and we will look at a number of them in these exercises.
They include:
- Repetition
  - Say the name out loud a few times
  - Write the name down a few times
- Association
  - Think about what you are most likely to remember about the person
  - Associate the name or person with a physical characteristic e.g. rosy cheeks; someone you know; a personal characteristic e.g. smiling Linda; a famous person; a rhyming word e.g. 'Phil' and 'hill'; an item; an occupation
  - Create a mind picture, the more unusual the better, e.g. imagine a large orange dinosaur wearing a baseball cap with the person's name on the cap

HOW TO PLAY

In this exercise, each person has an item that can act as a visual stimulus. The name of the item also begins with the first letter of the person's name.

Study the people, remember the names then turn over and fill in the sheet.

| **Eve** | **Cameron** | **Rosie** | **Gordon** |
| Earrings | Cap | Ribbons | Glasses |

REMEMBERING NAMES AND FACES 1

These are the four people:

 ROSIE

 GORDON

 EVE

 CAMERON

CORRECTING SPELLING 1

HOW TO PLAY

Rewrite the passage, correcting any spelling mistakes.

Yestarday I went too the mall. One of the chane stores had a twenty pur cent off sail.

The asistant showd me the latest range of leather bags and suitecases.

As I travell a lot I allways need a suiteable colection of bags and cases.

The case needs too be sturdy, lightwait and strong.

The hand lugage needs to be flexable, with many compartaments and zipped pockits.

Brown or biege is my prefered color.

The adjoinning store sold perfoume, whitch I bought for my neice.

I dicided to go too the bookstore, picked up severel guidbooks and biographys, then went to the checkout.

WORDSEARCH 1

STRAIGHTFORWARD

HOW TO PLAY

Words are placed in the grid vertically, horizontally or diagonally.

O	T	I	M	E	T	A	B	L	E
D	A	R	R	I	V	A	L	R	F
E	S	E	O	V	P	L	G	E	M
P	S	N	F	S	E	A	T	G	N
A	F	I	T	V	C	D	U	N	T
R	T	A	A	N	K	A	H	E	R
T	O	R	L	M	R	O	K	S	A
U	T	T	P	D	F	C	L	S	C
R	Y	A	W	L	I	A	R	A	K
E	N	O	I	T	A	T	S	P	O

ARRIVAL

DEPARTURE

GUARD

PASSENGER

PLATFORM

RAILWAY

SEAT

STATION

TICKET

TIMETABLE

TRACK

TRAIN

TRAVEL

WORD LADDER 1

HOW TO PLAY

Turn the first word into the last word by changing a single letter each time, making sure each step is a proper word.

The clues for each step are given.

LINE	
	Narrow road
	Ground
	Allow use of
	To guide
READ	

CONTINUOUS WORDS 1

HOW TO PLAY

This is a list of names joined together, with the word spaces removed. How many can you find?

Topic: Items that can be blue

jeanscornflowerindigoirissapphireeyesdeni

mribandglassagapanthusblueberryturquoise

paintshoesuniformcrayonbluebellbutterflyast

erangelfishsharkribbonpenmarkerfabricdelph

iniumpaperoceanflagstampsjayseainkskywh

aledyecarpufferfishlightshirtwoollapislazuli

WEB WORDS 1

HOW TO PLAY

Fill in each blank square with two letters to form a six letter word with the letters diagonally above and below. The words read downwards.

For example:

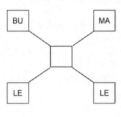

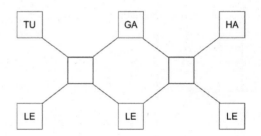

Becomes:

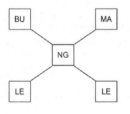

WORD CHAIN 1

HOW TO PLAY

Using one of the words, you have a minute to form a word chain by changing one letter at a time.

Repeat words are not counted.

For example, if the word were YET, your chain might be:

YES, YEW, FEW, FEE, SEE, TEE, TEN, HEN, PEN, PEG, PIG, RIG, RAG, RAT

If you come to a point where you are unable to make any more words, you can cross off the last word(s) and go back until you can continue the chain, as long as it is within the time limit.

Take a minute for each of the five words.

COW	
HEN	
PUT	
ATE	
AIR	

SOLVING SENTENCES 1

HOW TO PLAY

What does this sentence say?

IWE NTTOV IS ITA DAMY ESTE
RDA YBU THE WASEL SEW
HERE.

TWISTER 1

HOW TO PLAY

Four words, each 6 letters long, fit into the grid, in a stepped format.

Two words go downwards and two upwards, with the middle letters being shared.

One letter is given.

If the grid and words were:

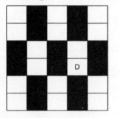

INURES, SEDATE

STADIA. STRUTS

The answer would be:

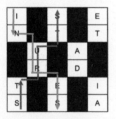

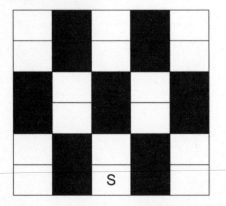

SKIMPY

STINKS

PANIER

REMITS

TEN ADJECTIVES 1

HOW TO PLAY

Think of 10 adjectives that start with the letters given.

FIRST LETTER 1

HOW TO PLAY

Change the first letter of each of the words in the group so that all words have the same, new, first letter. Make sure that the new words are proper words, though not proper nouns.

When you have found all the new letters, rearrange them to form a three-letter word.

	NEW LETTER
HILT - WEEP - DALE - SING - BEEN	
FLIGHT - CLONE - SUCTION - FIR - GRID	
BEAT - GALE - WAND - VOLE - LIGHT	

Word:

PATTERNS 1

HOW TO PLAY

Can you work out the pattern?

At the top of the first three columns is a name.

In the right hand column are three words that fit into the named categories.

Work out the pattern and place the words into the appropriate boxes in the grid. The first two have been done for you.

SAM	KEN	JIM	category	
			Name of wife	GILL KATH JESS
			Favorite type of tree	YEW FIR PALM
	VEST		Favorite type of clothing	HAT SHIRT VEST
			Favorite color	RED BLACK PINK
LAMB			Favorite animal	PIG LAMB HEN

LETTER SQUARES 1

HOW TO PLAY

Choose words that form a square going clockwise: Take the last letter of the given word, and write in a word of the same length starting with this letter and going downwards. Take the last letter of this word and write in another word starting with this letter and going to the left. Finally, take the last letter of this word and write in a word starting with this letter and ending with the first letter of the first word.

For example, if the first was SIT

You may add the words TON NOW and WAS to make

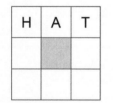

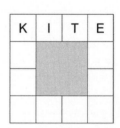

FICTIONAL LANGUAGE 1

HOW TO PLAY

A few words have been translated from English into a fictional language

Learn the translated words, then turn the page and fill in the fictional words in the gaps.

English	Fictional language
HOUR	ORASKAPAN
MIDNIGHT	HATIGABI
BOOK	AKLIBRO

FICTIONAL LANGUAGE 1

Text

It was the best thriller he had ever read and he could hardly put the

_____ down.

He turned the pages quickly, reading for hour after _____, not even noticing when the clock chimed

_____.

MISSING LETTERS 1

HOW TO PLAY

There are two 9-letter words, both of which read from left to right, with the words going upwards or downwards.

Some of the letters have been taken out and are listed on the right hand side. Can you put them in the correct places?

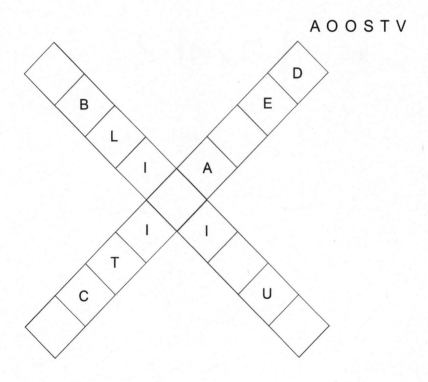

Level 2

WORD TRAIL 2

HOW TO PLAY

Find the 8 words listed in the grid starting with the circled letters.
Words go horizontally or vertically.

Ⓦ	E	N	I	Ⓢ	U
I	N	D	H	S	N
I	A	Ⓡ	G	I	Ⓜ
N	Ⓢ	Ⓕ	O	S	E
E	L	R	O	T	C
E	T	Ⓕ	S	T	Ⓘ

FOG

FROST

ICE

MIST

RAIN

SLEET

SUNSHINE

WIND

JOINING WORDS 2

HOW TO PLAY

Find a word that completes the first word and begins the second.

The number in brackets indicates the number of letters that are missing.

TRA	__ __	SERT	(2)
BO	__ __	TEND	(2)
PLA	__ __	ARLY	(2)
TRA	__ __ __	VET	(3)
HO	__ __ __	EVISE	(3)
TIC	__ __ __	TLE	(3)
PASS	__ __ __ __	RAIT	(4)
BOO	__ __ __ __	PIN	(4)
IS	__ __ __ __	ING	(4)

PYRAMID WORDS 2

HOW TO PLAY

Fill in the rows with 1-letter through to 10-letter words that begin with the letter A

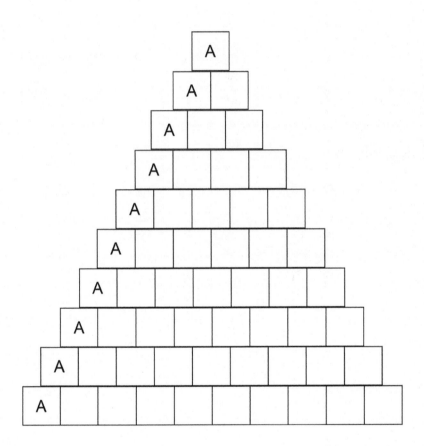

LETTER CROSS 2

HOW TO PLAY

Cross out the letters that appear twice.

The remaining letters spell the name of a chemical element.

G	I	V		N	P	Q	C
Q	Z	X	W	S	J	Y	R
B	J	L	P	A	W	E	T
H	R	F	M	H	Z	U	G
A	K	N		X	E	C	Y
T	F	D	B	O	V	L	K

SPEED WORDS 2

HOW TO PLAY

Choose 10 words that fit the criteria given.

Choose words that are not proper nouns.

Use a different word for each question.

Choose a word that:		
1	Has 3 letters in alphabetical order	
2	Rhymes with "CLOTHES	
3	Had 5 letters and ends in "C"	
4	Has 6 letters and starts with "V"	
5	Has 2 syllables and starts with "Y"	
6	Fits into "D __ V __ __ E".	
7	Is an anagram of "GOLOI"	
8	Has 4 letters and starts with a double letter	
9	Is an anagram of "MEAT" and "TEAM"	
10	Has 2 syllables and starts with "Z"	

WORKING IT OUT 2

HOW TO PLAY

Work out what is unusual about this passage.

"All boys can dance, even Freddie" Georgina heartily insisted.

"Jeff, Katherine left Maria's nephew outside Pablo's! Quick, run!" shouted Theo urgently.

"Very well!" Xavier yelled zestfully.

X WORDS 2

HOW TO PLAY

Place the correct words in the rows in the grid so that both diagonals spell a four-letter word reading from top to bottom.

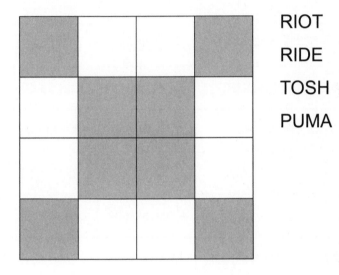

RIOT

RIDE

TOSH

PUMA

SYNONYMS 2

HOW TO PLAY

Find the ten matching pairs of synonyms in the grid.

Rearrange the four remaining words to form a sentence

JOURNEY	INSTRUCTOR	SOLIDER	BUILDING
DISEASE	YOUR	IMPEDIMENT	COLLEAGUE
KINSFOLK	HERMIT	GRASS	AILMENT
CO WORKER	BRAIN	FAMILY	RECLUSE
LAWN	VOYAGE	EDUCATOR	LOOK
AFTER	HINDRANCE	WARRIOR	EDIFICE

Sentence: _____ _____

_____ _____

FIRST AND LAST LETTERS 2

HOW TO PLAY

Think of 10 words where the first and last letters alternate.

For example, if the first word is 'REALLY', the next word would need to start with Y and end with R, the third word would then start with R and end with Y again, and so on.

Example: REALLY – YOUR – RAY – YONDER – RARITY – YEAR – RATIFY – YOUNGER – ROMANY – YOUNGSTER

Using the given words, find another 9 words with alternating first and last letters.

For words ending in S, aim to avoid using plurals.

COUNT	
HINT	
EVEN	

SPLIT WORDS 2

HOW TO PLAY

There are eight 4-letter words that have been split into 2-letter pieces.

Find the matching parts of the eight words.

Topic: Parts of the body

CH	KN	NO	IN
SE	CA	NE	HE
OT	AD	ND	LF
HA	EE	CK	FO

1. _____
2. _____
3. _____
4. _____
5. _____
6. _____
7. _____
8. _____

MEMORY GRID 2

HOW TO PLAY

Study the grid, and remember the position of the words.

Then turn the page and answer the questions.

Topic: Animals

		CAT		
		SHEEP		
PIG	DOG	OX	MOOSE	HORSE
		BULL		
		BEAR		

MEMORY GRID 2
Questions

1. Which animal is directly below BULL?

2. Which animal is at the opposite end of the row to PIG?

3. Which animal is two spaces to the right of DOG?

4. Which animal is between SHEEP and BULL?

5. Which animal is directly above SHEEP?

DEFINITIONS 2

HOW TO PLAY

Choose the correct definition for each word.

Oblique
To legally bind
Slanting
Hidden and remote

Squire
Country gentleman
A county
A title for gentleman

Vapid
Empty
Insipid, flat
Moisture

Scimitar
Sparkle
Synopsis, outline
Oriental curved sword

Fez
Conical red cap with tassel
To confess
Festival

Bittern
Tasting like quinine
Small carplike fish
Marsh bird

Conch
Shellfish
Easy task
Composition for solo instrument

Meander
Significance
Wander at random
Lacking

Nook
Strip of dough
Secluded corner
Nape of the neck

Judder
Being characteristic of Jewish people
Perform conjuring tricks
Shake noisily or violently

COLUMN WORDS 2

HOW TO PLAY

Place the words in the correct rows in the grid so that columns 2 and 5 spell out six-letter words.

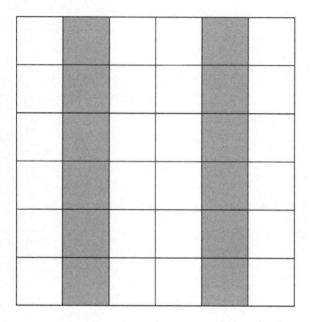

BUTANE

INCISE

OSMIUM

ERBIUM

ATRIAL

CAMERA

STRINGS 2

HOW TO PLAY

The grid has 30 boxes.

Place words in the boxes, where the last letter of one becomes the first letter of the next. The words must fit exactly into the 30 boxes. Use any words you like

For example:

H	O	U	S	E	L	E	P	H	A	N	T	O	W	E	R	I

N	G	A	R	D	E	N	E	T	T	L	E	S

(HOUSE, ELEPHANT, TOWER, RING, GARDEN, NETTLES)

COMBINED ANAGRAMS 2

HOW TO PLAY

Two words have been combined and their letters arranged in alphabetical order.

Can you work out the two words?

For example the words SEVEN and EIGHT would combine to form EEEGHINSTV

Topic: Animals

	Answer
EGIILNORT	
EGIKMNOPY	
ACEFLLMOW	

QUOTE GRID 2

HOW TO PLAY

Included in the grid is a one sentence quote. The words are in a continuous string, and the first word has been circled.

When you have found the quote, put the small letters from each square in the correct order into the empty grid to find a phrase relating to the quote

G PROBLEMS	A THE	M NEAR	R (THE)
I OF		U PROBLEMS	S VERY
C LIFE.	B OF	I PUZZLES	K ARE

WORD CAPSULE 2

HOW TO PLAY

Choose six 5-letter words that start with the letter on the left and end with the letters on the right. Choose a different word each time.

For example if the capsule was:

H				C
				L
				O
				U
				D
				Y

Your answers may be:

H	A	V	O	C
	O	V	E	L
	E	L	L	O
	A	I	K	U
	A	T	E	D
	U	R	R	Y

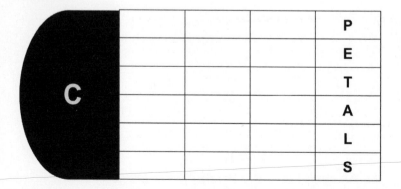

C				P
				E
				T
				A
				L
				S

60

MISSING ALPHABET 2

HOW TO PLAY

All 26 letters of the alphabet have been removed from this passage.

Can you put them in the correct places?

The alphabet is listed so you can cross off each letter as you place it into the passage

When __anuel knoc__ed on __he doo__ he __eard a

gro__ling soun__.

He __umped ner__ously, __uestioning wh__ he was

th__re. __ould it __e a griz__ly be__r? An__iously he

__istened to the gr__wls.

He heard lo__d __ootsteps. The door wa__ flun__

ope__ and a t__ny man looked u__ at him.

ABCDEFGHIJKLMNOPQRSTUVWXYZ

MINI WORD SUDOKU 2

HOW TO PLAY

Place the letters from the 6-letter word **METHOD** in the grid so that each column, each row, and each of the six 2×3 sub-grids contains all of the 6 letters from the word.

		O			
		H	E	T	
M	E		T		
				H	T
				D	

WORDS FROM A WORD 2

HOW TO PLAY

Choose words that begin with the given letters and fit the category.
For example if the grid contained:

LETTER	CATEGORY	NUMBER OF WORDS
K	Girl's name	1
E	Occupation	2
N	Place name	3
T	Adjective	4

You would need to think of 1 girl's name beginning with K;
2 occupations beginning with; E, 3 place names beginning with N;
4 adjectives beginning with T.

LETTER	CATEGORY	NUMBER OF WORDS	WORDS
A	Flower	1	
U	Adjective	2	
S	Clothing	3	
T	Food	4	
I	Place	5	
N	Boy's name	6	

RHYMING WORDS 2

HOW TO PLAY

Find a word that rhymes with the given word and fits the definition.
For example:

WORD	DEFINITION
BARROW	Vegetable

The answer would be
MARROW

WORD	DEFINITION	RHYMING WORD
STEAK	Prolonged pain	
TALK	Loud harsh cry	
JOKE	Noise made by amphibian	
DUNK	Religious man	
BIRCH	Religious building	
RED	Fear	
THIRD	Group of animals	
SIGHED	Scold	
SQUAD	Incline head slightly	
SWORD	Criminal deception	

NAMES 2

HOW TO PLAY

Each row has a five-letter boy's name in it with the letters rearranged, plus one extra letter.

Work out the name, then place the extra letter in the right hand column.

Rearrange the extra letters to make another name.

For example:

						Boy's name	Extra letter
E	C	F	A	L	N	LANCE	F

						Boy's name	Extra letter
F	F	E	G	A	O		
C	A	R	S	A	I		
P	R	T	E	W	E		
S	R	O	I	B	E		
H	N	I	R	C	S		
R	A	D	S	O	C		
Additional name							

REMEMBERING NAMES AND FACES 2

There are various strategies for remembering names and faces and we will look at a number of them in these exercises.

They include:

- Repetition
    - Say the name out loud a few times
    - Write the name down a few times
- Association
    - Think about what you are most likely to remember about the person.
    - Associate the name or person with a physical characteristic e.g. rosy cheeks; someone you know; a personal characteristic e.g. smiling Linda; a famous person; a rhyming word e.g. 'Phil' and 'hill'; an item; an occupation.
    - Create a mind picture, the more unusual the better, e.g. imagine a large orange dinosaur wearing a baseball cap with the person's name on the cap

HOW TO PLAY

In this exercise, each person has an item that can act as a visual stimulus. The name of the item also begins with the first letter of the person's name.

Study the people, remember the names then turn over and fill in the sheet.

Henry

Terry

Nancy

Frances

Scott

Brenda

66

REMEMBERING NAMES AND FACES 2

These are the six people:

CORRECTING SPELLING 2

HOW TO PLAY

Rewrite the passage, correcting any spelling mistakes.

My farther is a grate exampel of how life should bee in retirment. He worked hard as a langauge teacher for allmost fourty years, and is now enjoiying a fullfilling retyrement.

My dad has many hobbeys; he has lots of freinds, and he has looked after his health well by having many activiteys.

His intrests include varios forms of danceing, caligraphy and philately (stamp colecting).

He keeps in reguler contact with all of his family, friends and acquaintences by phone or email. He is generouse with his time and money, constently wiling to help others and do favours for them.

He is also fun to be around as he is a great raconture.

WORD SEARCH 2

'ANT' WORDS

HOW TO PLAY

Words are placed in the grid vertically, horizontally or diagonally.

All words contain the letters 'ANT'

P	E	U	Q	I	T	N	A	Q	D
R	L	G	R	A	N	T	E	D	E
E	B	A	N	T	E	R	A	R	C
C	T	P	N	C	G	T	N	E	A
A	R	N	D	T	N	P	T	T	N
N	G	Q	A	A	E	R	I	A	T
T	P	D	C	D	B	D	C	E	E
M	I	S	C	R	E	A	N	T	R
B	E	B	R	Q	G	P	R	N	B
D	E	P	O	L	E	T	N	A	P

ANTEATER

ANTELOPE

ANTIC

ANTIQUE

BANTER

DECANTER

GRANTED

PLANTED

DESCANT

MISCREANT

PEDANT

RECANT

WORD LADDER 2

HOW TO PLAY

Turn the first word into the last word by changing a single letter each time, making sure each step is a proper word.

The clues for each step are given.

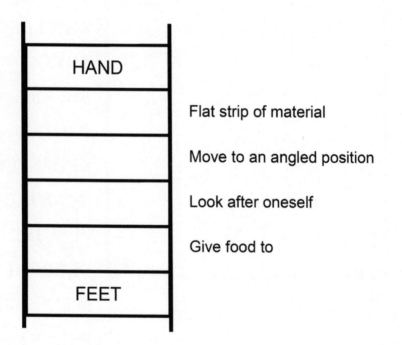

HAND

Flat strip of material

Move to an angled position

Look after oneself

Give food to

FEET

CONTINUOUS WORDS 2

HOW TO PLAY

This is a list of names joined together, with the word spaces removed. How many can you find?

Topic: Birds

bluebirdmeadowlarkgodwittealternmockingbirdduck
yellowhammerkingfisherbustarddabchickkiwiibiscuck
ooospreyfalconparakeetrobinalbatrosssaddlebackswi
ftoystercatchertomtitthrushheronostrichvulturerheago
ldfinchhawkwrencassowarygrebecormorantshoebillfl
amingoquailcondoreaglepelicancraneemurailploverp
etrellapwinggullfinch

WEB WORDS 2

HOW TO PLAY

Fill in each blank square with two letters to form a six letter word with the letters diagonally above and below. The words read downwards.

For example:

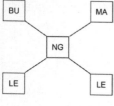

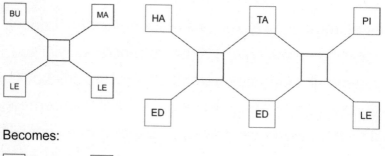

Becomes:

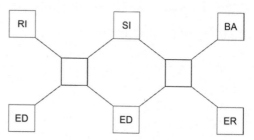

WORD CHAIN 2

HOW TO PLAY

Using one of the words, you have a minute to form a word chain by changing one letter at a time.

Repeat words are not counted.

For example, if the word were YET, your chain might be:

YES, YEW, FEW, FEE, SEE, TEE, TEN, HEN, PEN, PEG, PIG, RIG, RAG, RAT

If you come to a point where you are unable to make any more words, you can cross off the last word(s) and go back until you can continue the chain, as long as it is within the time limit.

Take a minute for each of the five words.

TAN	
SEE	
TOO	
ILL	
PAY	

SOLVING SENTENCES 2

HOW TO PLAY

What does this sentence say?

ADNAGU DNA AYNEK SI SA
ROTAUQE EHT NO SI AILAMOS

TWISTER 2

HOW TO PLAY

Six words, each 6 letters long, fit into the grid, in a stepped format.

Three words go downwards and three upwards, with the middle letters being shared.

One letter is given.

If the grid and words were:

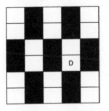

INURES, SEDATE
STADIA. STRUTS

The answer would be:

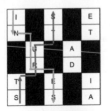

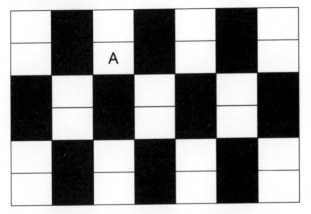

RABBIT
ELATED
COLLAR
TITANS
RABBLE
DOLLAR

TEN ADJECTIVES 2

HOW TO PLAY

Think of 10 adjectives that start with the letters given.

C	
G	

FIRST LETTER 2

HOW TO PLAY

Change the first letter of each of the words in the group so that all words have the same, new, first letter. Make sure that the new words are proper words, though not proper nouns.

When you have found all the new letters, rearrange them to form a three-letter word.

	NEW LETTER
FREAK - DIRE - THINE - HAD - BOMB	
BAT - GRANGE - EVEN - SPINE - ETHER	
HOWL - OUR - LOOP - BELL - TABLE	

Word: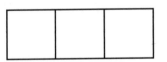

PATTERNS 2

HOW TO PLAY

Can you work out the pattern?

At the top of the first three columns is a name.

In the right hand column are three words that fit into the named categories.

Work out the pattern and place the words into the appropriate boxes in the grid. The first two have been done for you.

ALAN	JAMES	JOSEPH	category	
			Name of wife	MARIA ANNE JANICE
			Favorite state	ALASKA TEXAS OHIO
BLUE			Favorite color	BLUE PURPLE GREEN
			Favorite food	CHEESE MEAT BREAD
		SKIING	Favorite sport	CHESS SKIING GOLF

LETTER SQUARES 2

HOW TO PLAY

Choose words that form a square going clockwise: Take the last letter of the given word, and write in a word of the same length starting with this letter and going downwards. Take the last letter of this word and write in another word starting with this letter and going to the left. Finally, take the last letter of this word and write in a word starting with this letter and ending with the first letter of the first word.

For example, if the first was SIT

You may add the words TON NOW and WAS to make

S	I	T

S	I	T
A		O
W	O	N

T	O	P

P	R	A	Y

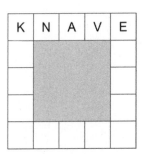

K	N	A	V	E

L	O	V	I	N	G

FICTIONAL LANGUAGE 2

HOW TO PLAY

A few words have been translated from English into a fictional language

Learn the translated words, then turn the page and fill in the fictional words in the gaps.

English	Fictional language
POPCORN	PAPMAI
CINEMA	SINESAFIL
SATURDAY	SABSEIJ

FICTIONAL LANGUAGE 2

Text

Kelly loved going to the _____,

especially on _____ nights with

her friends.

They would buy their tickets and some

_____ and settle down to

watch the film.

MISSING LETTERS 2

HOW TO PLAY

There are two 9-letter words, both of which read from left to right, with the words going upwards or downwards.

Some of the letters have been taken out and are listed on the right hand side. Can you put them in the correct places?

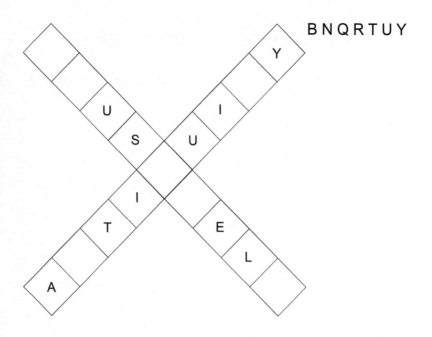

BNQRTUY

Level 3

WORD TRAIL 3

HOW TO PLAY

Find the 6 words listed in the grid starting with the circled letters.
Words go horizontally or vertically.

N	D	(S)	W	E	D
A	L	G	(N)	N	E
Y	(F)	N	O	R	Y
L	R	(E)	E	W	A
A	A	N	C	L	O
T	(I)	D	N	A	(P)

ENGLAND

FRANCE

ITALY

NORWAY

POLAND

SWEDEN

JOINING WORDS 3

HOW TO PLAY

Find a word that completes the first word and begins the second.

The number in brackets indicates the number of letters that are missing.

LUP	_ _	SIDE	(2)
PYL	_ _	ION	(2)
THRE	_ _	TEND	(2)
CAR	_ _ _	AL	(3)
FRI	_ _ _	ING	(3)
MOT	_ _ _	RING	(3)
STU	_ _ _ _	IST	(4)
INTE	_ _ _ _	FUL	(4)
UNDER	_ _ _ _	SOME	(4)

PYRAMID WORDS 3

HOW TO PLAY

Fill in the rows with words starting with the letters given.

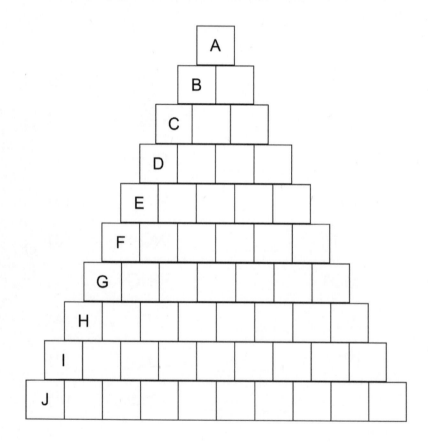

LETTER CROSS 3

HOW TO PLAY

Cross out the letters that appear twice.

The remaining letters spell the name of an occupation.

P	Z	G	O	H	M	E	T
	B	A	X	I	J	N	X
S	W	Q	C	O	D	C	V
N	D	H	U	K	Q	F	J
U	F	T	I	Z	B	P	
L	M	G	V	K	R	Y	S

SPEED WORDS 3

HOW TO PLAY

Choose 10 words that fit the criteria given.

Choose words that are not proper nouns.

Use a different word for each question.

Choose a word that:		
1	Has 3 letters, 2 of which are vowels	
2	Fits into "A __ __ __ E"	
3	Is an anagram of "NOGEAR"	
4	Has 1 syllable and rhymes with "SOUP"	
5	Has 6 letters including "BB"	
6	Ends in "CKY"	
7	Has 5 letters and starts with "Q"	
8	Has two lots of double letters	
9	Has 2 syllables and ends in "L"	
10	Has a "W" in the middle	

WORKING IT OUT 3

HOW TO PLAY

Work out what is unusual about this passage.

"Try not to worry?" pouts Troy, "Trust you? Your story's worn out. No sun, no snow, no sport."

"Sprouts, quorn, or soup?" purrs Suzy.

"Stop your pow wow" tuts Poppy. "You two, trot up to town . . . now!"

X WORDS 3

HOW TO PLAY

Place the correct words in the rows in the grid so that both diagonals spell a four-letter word reading from top to bottom.

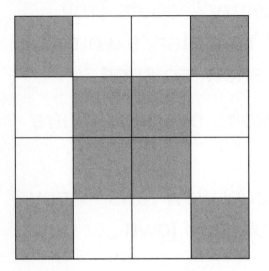

SETS

ELSE

FAYS

VERY

SYNONYMS 3

HOW TO PLAY

Find the ten matching pairs of synonyms in the grid.

Rearrange the four remaining words to form a sentence

PERSON	SEAT	PARCEL	ROBBER
MINUTES	MIST	INSECT	PRESENTATION
HOUSE	THIEF	USE	CLOTH
PACKET	HUMAN	WELL	FOG
MATERIAL	SPEECH	HOME	DAWN
SUNRISE	CHAIR	FIVE	BUG

Sentence: _____ _____

_____ _____

FIRST AND LAST LETTERS 3

HOW TO PLAY

Think of 10 words where the first and last letters alternate.

For example, if the first word is 'REALLY', the next word would need to start with Y and end with R, the third word would then start with R and end with Y again, and so on.

Example: REALLY – YOUR – RAY – YONDER – RARITY – YEAR – RATIFY – YOUNGER – ROMANY – YOUNGSTER

Using the given words, find another 9 words with alternating first and last letters.

For words ending in S, aim to avoid using plurals.

SOUP	
RACING	
MAIL	

SPLIT WORDS 3

HOW TO PLAY

There are eight 4-letter words that have been split into 2-letter pieces.

Find the matching parts of the eight words.

Topic: Food

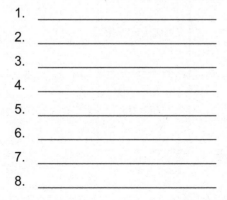

RT	BE	KE	PL
RK	VE	RI	CA
CE	TA	UM	PO
AR	EF	PE	AL

1. _____
2. _____
3. _____
4. _____
5. _____
6. _____
7. _____
8. _____

MEMORY GRID 3

HOW TO PLAY

Study the grid, and remember the position of the words.

Then turn the page and answer the questions.

Topic: Musical instruments

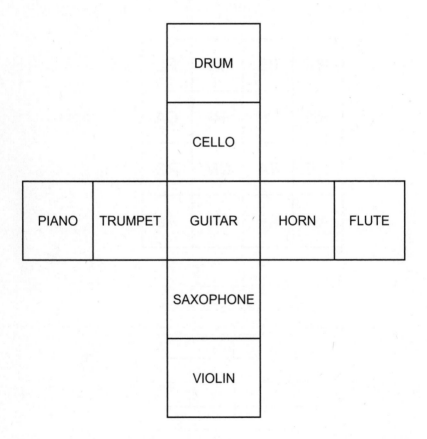

MEMORY GRID 3

Questions

1. Which instrument is in the center of the grid?

2. Which instrument is second from bottom?

3. Which instrument is two places to the right of TRUMPET?

4. Which instrument is directly below DRUM?

5. Which instrument is immediately to the right of HORN?

COLUMN WORDS 3

HOW TO PLAY

Place the words in the correct rows in the grid so that columns 2 and 5 spell out six-letter words.

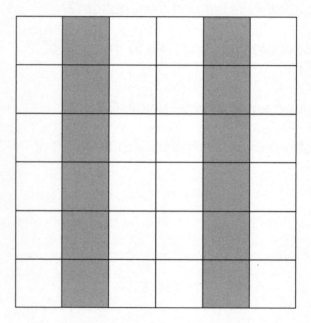

AVIARY

UNDONE

LOOFAH

IGNITE

CLASPS

BILLET

DEFINITIONS 3

HOW TO PLAY

Choose the correct definition for each word.

Phoenix
Distinct units of sound that separate one word from another
A mythical bird burned in a funeral pyre, born again from the ashes
Not genuine

Rejoinder
A quick or witty reply
A feeling of great joy
To meet up with long lost acquaintances

Swarthy
Full of machinery filings
Inclined to show off
Having a dark skin

Triathlon
The process of assessing the seriousness of illnesses
An event in which horses or dogs compete
An athletic contest involving three events

Weevil
Small beetle with a long snout
Immoral and wicked
Machine for producing fabric

Liana
A go-between
A climbing plant that hangs from trees in tropical forests
In a direct line of ancestry

Serge
Sudden powerful force or upward movement
A rank of noncommissioned officer
Hard wearing woollen fabric

Quark
Imitation meat mycoprotein
Group of subatomic particles
A peculiar habit

Histrionic
Excessively dramatic
Belonging to, or set in the past
Branch of biology concerned with the microscopic structure of tissues

Importunate
Very persistent
Able to transfer data into a computer file
Regrettable or inappropriate

STRINGS 3

HOW TO PLAY

The grid has 30 boxes.

Place words in the boxes, where the last letter of one becomes the first letter of the next. The words must fit exactly into the 30 boxes.

The theme is 'place names'. All words placed in the grid must be names of places.

For example:

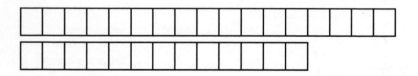

C	H	I	N	A	M	S	T	E	R	D	A	M	A	D	R	I

D	E	N	M	A	R	K	A	M	P	A	L	A

(CHINA, AMSTERDAM, MADRID, DENMARK, KAMPALA)

COMBINED ANAGRAMS 3

HOW TO PLAY

Two words have been combined and their letters arranged in alphabetical order.

Can you work out the two words?

For example the words SEVEN and EIGHT would combine to form EEEGHINSTV

Topic: Colors

	Answer
ADEEGNORR	
BBELNORWU	
AEGLPPRRUY	

QUOTE GRID 3

HOW TO PLAY

Included in the grid is a one sentence quote. The words are in a continuous string, and the first word has been circled.

When you have found the quote, put the small letters from each square in the correct order into the empty grid to find a phrase relating to the quote.

S	K	G	A	U
OUR	DEEP	BECAUSE	LANGUAGE	DEVELOPED

I	E		L	G
INNER	OF		I	WE

L	L	S	N	A
DESIRE	TO	COMPLAIN.	BELIEVE	PERSONALLY

WORD CAPSULE 3

HOW TO PLAY

Choose six 5-letter words that start with the letter on the left and end with the letters on the right. Choose a different word each time.

For example if the capsule was:

H				C
				L
				O
				U
				D
				Y

Your answers may be:

H	A	V	O	C
	O	V	E	L
	E	L	L	O
	A	I	K	U
	A	T	E	D
	U	R	R	Y

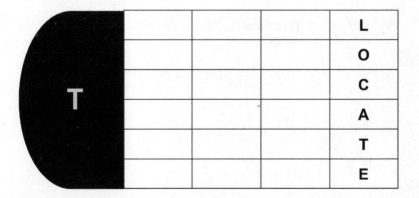

T				L
				O
				C
				A
				T
				E

MISSING ALPHABET 3

HOW TO PLAY

All 26 letters of the alphabet have been removed from this passage.

Can you put them in the correct places?

The alphabet is listed so you can cross off each letter as you place it into the passage

Manuel loo__ed do__n at t__e tiny man. He was

weari__g enormo__s ho__nailed bo__ts. He al__o had

a __ery stran__e e__pression on his __ace.

"Hel__o" s__ueaked Manuel timi__ly. "I __ust want__d

to ask if __ou h__ve a gri__zly bea__ in your

apar__ment?" he added feel__ng e__barrassed.

"Ste__ inside" the tiny man __ommanded.

ABCDEFGHIJKLMNOPQRSTUVWXYZ

MINI WORD SUDOKU 3

HOW TO PLAY

Place the letters from the 6-letter word **PHRASE** in the grid so that each column, each row, and each of the six 2×3 sub-grids contains all of the 6 letters from the word.

	S			H	
A			R		
E			P		
		A	S		
		R			

WORDS FROM A WORD 3

HOW TO PLAY

Choose words that begin with the given letters and fit the category.
For example if the grid contained:

LETTER	CATEGORY	NUMBER OF WORDS
K	Girl's name	1
E	Occupation	2
N	Place name	3
T	Adjective	4

You would need to think of 1 girl's name beginning with K; 2
occupations beginning with; E, 3 place names beginning with N; 4
adjectives beginning with T.

LETTER	CATEGORY	NUMBER OF WORDS	WORDS
M	Color	1	
A	Food	2	
D	Creature	3	
R	Surname of famous person	4	
I	Girl's name	5	
D	Activity	6	

RHYMING WORDS 3

HOW TO PLAY

Find a word that rhymes with the given word and fits the definition.

For example:

WORD	DEFINITION
BARROW	Vegetable

The answer would be
MARROW

WORD	DEFINITION	RHYMING WORD
CLAY	Sound made by horse	
CHAIR	Mammal with short tail and long ears	
QUAY	Joint in body	
WEANED	Mischievous person	
SPIRE	Singers	
HOOT	Fibre from plant	
THOUGH	Enemy	
TOWER	Of acid taste	
BLONDE	Slender rod carried in hand	
WHO	In accordance with actual state of affairs	

NAMES 3

HOW TO PLAY

Each row has a five-letter girl's name in it with the letters rearranged, plus one extra letter.

Work out the name, then place the extra letter in the right hand column.

Rearrange the extra letters to make another name.

For example:

						Girl's name	Extra letter
M	A	M	E	S	G	GEMMA	S

						Girl's name	Extra letter
A	R	S	C	O	L		
Y	L	L	E	P	O		
H	I	D	E	N	A		
Z	L	H	A	I	E		
F	A	I	S	O	A		
G	E	L	R	C	A		
Additional name							

REMEMBERING NAMES AND FACES 3

There are various strategies for remembering names and faces and we will look at a number of them in these exercises.
They include:

*   Repetition
    *   Say the name out loud a few times
    *   Write the name down a few times
*   Association
    *   Think about what you are most likely to remember about the person
    *   Associate the name or person with a physical characteristic e.g. rosy cheeks; someone you know; a personal characteristic e.g. smiling Linda; a famous person; a rhyming word e.g. 'Phil' and 'hill'; an item; an occupation
    *   Create a mind picture, the more unusual the better, e.g. imagine a large orange dinosaur wearing a baseball cap with the person's name on the cap

HOW TO PLAY

In this exercise, try a rhyming strategy to help you remember. For example 'Marty likes to party', 'Pat likes her cat'.

Study the people, remember the names then turn over and fill in the sheet.

Dave   Kate   Mike

Sue   Ted   Lynn

REMEMBERING NAMES AND FACES 3

These are the six people:

CORRECTING SPELLING 3

HOW TO PLAY

Rewrite the passage, correcting any spelling mistakes.

Maria had been reeding a horor story about a woman in a foriegn country who had been atacked by an amature criminal.

Strange and wierd ocurrences had been hapening to the woman and she felt harased and scared.

Thunder and lightening seemd to be a reguler wether pattern, makeing the electrical equipement malfunction.

She herd frightning laugheter comeing from the next apartment, and was sure she spyed anouther man carrying a knaife.

She siezed the vegtable cutter, greatful that it had been sharpend, and peeped out of the window.

They're was definately a second man.

WORDSEARCH 3
SIMILAR WORDS

HOW TO PLAY

Words are placed in the grid vertically, horizontally or diagonally.

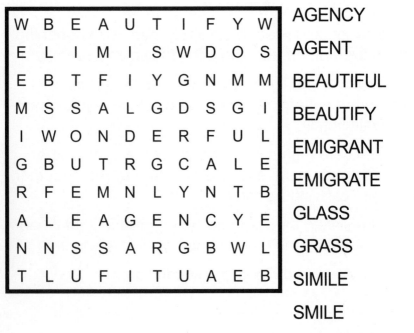

W	B	E	A	U	T	I	F	Y	W
E	L	I	M	I	S	W	D	O	S
E	B	T	F	I	Y	G	N	M	M
M	S	S	A	L	G	D	S	G	I
I	W	O	N	D	E	R	F	U	L
G	B	U	T	R	G	C	A	L	E
R	F	E	M	N	L	Y	N	T	B
A	L	E	A	G	E	N	C	Y	E
N	N	S	S	A	R	G	B	W	L
T	L	U	F	I	T	U	A	E	B

AGENCY

AGENT

BEAUTIFUL

BEAUTIFY

EMIGRANT

EMIGRATE

GLASS

GRASS

SIMILE

SMILE

WONDERFUL

WONDERMENT

WORD LADDER 3

HOW TO PLAY

Turn the first word into the last word by changing a single letter each time, making sure each step is a proper word.

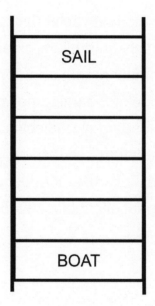

CONTINUOUS WORDS 3

HOW TO PLAY

This is a list of names joined together, with the word spaces removed. How many can you find?

Topic: Vegetables

potatookraartichokeendiveceleriaccornbrus
selssproutsspinachkohlrabilentilsleekkalelettucecala
breseceleryyammushroommangetouttaroonionnavyb
eansshallotturnippintobeanspumpkinturnipparsnipred
pepperrutabagaasparagusradicchiobokchoybroccolic
auliflowerradishbutternutsquashzucchinigarlicchardc
arroteggplantwasabijerusalemartichokepeascabbage
cucumberchickpeasalfalfablackeyedpeas

WEB WORDS 3

HOW TO PLAY

Fill in each blank square with two letters to form a six letter word with the letters diagonally above and below. The words read downwards.

For example:

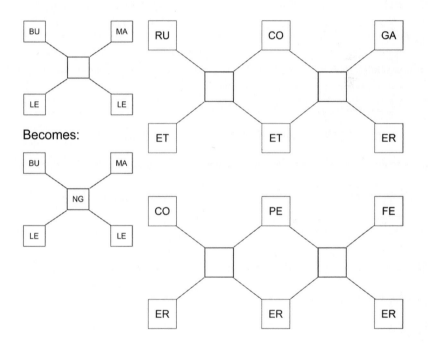

Becomes:

WORD CHAIN 3

HOW TO PLAY

Using one of the words, you have a minute to form a word chain by changing one letter at a time.

Repeat words are not counted.

For example, if the word were SAME, your chain might be:

FAME, TAME, TALE, TAKE, CAKE, RAKE, RAVE, RAGE, CAGE, CAVE, HAVE, GAVE, GATE, LATE, MATE, MOTE, NOTE, NOSE, ROSE, ROTE

If you come to a point where you are unable to make any more words, you can cross off the last word(s) and go back until you can continue the chain, as long as it is within the time limit.

Take a minute for each of the five words.

SILL	
DARE	
CODE	
WORD	
MUST	

SOLVING SENTENCES 3

HOW TO PLAY

What does this sentence say?

YT LUCI FFIDEL TTILH TIWSELZ ZUPFOSDNI
KESEHT TUOKRO WOTELBA ERAD NATNEG
ILLETNIY LHGIHE RAEL POE PEMOS

TWISTER 3

HOW TO PLAY

Six words, each 6 letters long, fit into the grid, in a stepped format.

Three words go downwards and two upwards, with the middle letters being shared.

One letter is given.

If the grid and words were:

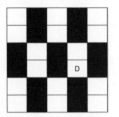

INURES, SEDATE

STADIA. STRUTS

The answer would be:

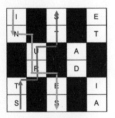

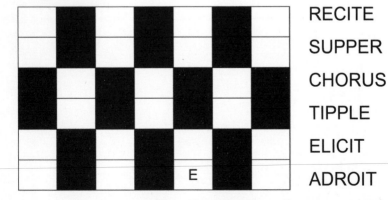

RECITE

SUPPER

CHORUS

TIPPLE

ELICIT

ADROIT

TEN ADJECTIVES 3

HOW TO PLAY

Think of 10 adjectives that start with the letters given.

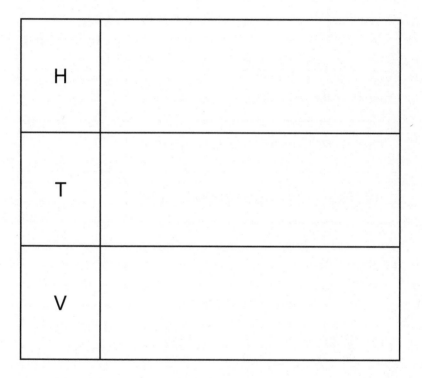

H	
T	
V	

FIRST LETTER 3

HOW TO PLAY

Change the first letter of each of the words in the group so that all words have the same, new, first letter. Make sure that the new words are proper words, though not proper nouns.

When you have found all the new letters, rearrange them to form a three-letter word.

	NEW LETTER
BEAR - HOUR - GET - FEW - SOUTH	
CAR - WILY - MUCH - YAK - DOZE	
WOKE - TOY - NEST - HAM - RIG	

Word:

PATTERNS 3

HOW TO PLAY

Can you work out the pattern?

At the top of the first three columns is a name.

In the right hand column are three words that fit into the named categories.

Work out the pattern and place the words into the appropriate boxes in the grid. The first two have been done for you.

PAM	SUSAN	CHRISTINA	category	
	FRANKLIN		Name of husband	TIMOTHY FRANKLIN GEORGE
			Favorite animal	ELEPHANT DOG LION
	ITALY		Favorite country	SPAIN ITALY HOLLAND
			Favorite fruit	ORANGE LIME BANANA
			Favorite film	LION KING STAR WARS DUNE

LETTER SQUARES 3

HOW TO PLAY

Choose words that form a square going clockwise: Take the last letter of the given word, and write in a word of the same length starting with this letter and going downwards. Take the last letter of this word and write in another word starting with this letter and going to the left. Finally, take the last letter of this word and write in a word starting with this letter and ending with the first letter of the first word.

For example, if the first was SIT

You may add the words TON NOW and WAS to make

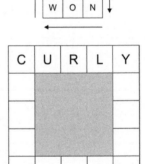

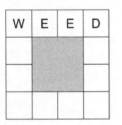

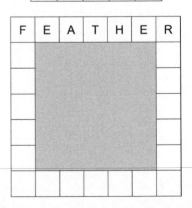

FICTIONAL LANGUAGE 3

HOW TO PLAY

A few words have been translated from English into a fictional language

Learn the translated words, then turn the page and fill in the fictional words in the gaps.

English	Fictional language
WISH	NAISDRE
RED	PULACRI
TRAIN	SERYETRA

FICTIONAL LANGUAGE 3
Text

Little Tommy's dream was to get a

_____ set for his birthday.

A big one with _____ carriages.

He lay in bed at night making a

_____ that it would come

true.

MISSING LETTERS 3

HOW TO PLAY

There are three 9-letter words, that read from left to right, with the words going upwards or downwards.

Some of the letters have been taken out and are listed on the right hand side. Can you put them in the correct places?

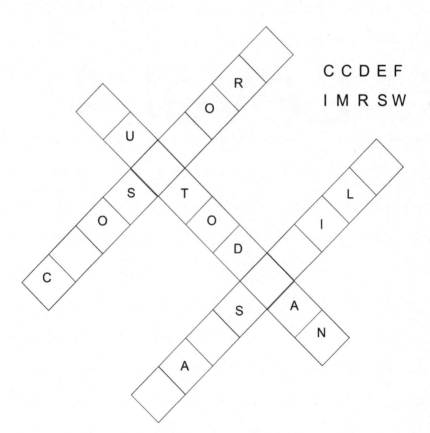

Level 4

WORD TRAIL 4

HOW TO PLAY

Find the 6 words listed in the grid starting with the circled letters.

Words go horizontally or vertically.

F	R	A	P	D	A
U	E	(H)	P	Y	L
L	E	H	(C)	Y	(G)
S	A	N	T	L	(J)
A	S	U	O	L	O
E	L	(P)	Y	O	(J)

CHEERFUL

GLAD

HAPPY

JOLLY

JOYOUS

PLEASANT

JOINING WORDS 4

HOW TO PLAY

Find a word that completes the first word and begins the second.

The number in brackets indicates the number of letters that are missing.

BAK	__ __	MINE	(2)
HAND	__ __	SSON	(2)
AM	__ __	TRY	(2)
GLO	__ __ __	ANCE	(3)
CLO	__ __ __	TLE	(3)
FAL	__ __ __	CERT	(3)
HALL	__ __ __ __	SMAN	(4)
RAIN	__ __ __ __	IBLE	(4)
ANI	__ __ __ __	LING	(4)

PYRAMID WORDS 4

HOW TO PLAY

Fill in the rows with words that include the letters given.

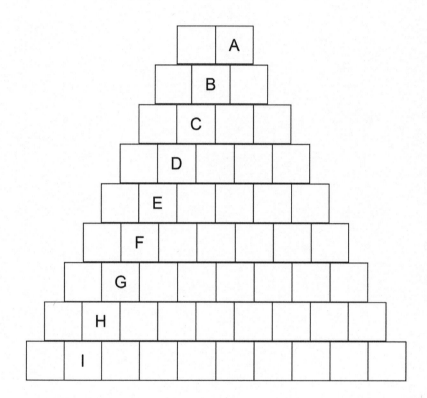

LETTER CROSS 4

HOW TO PLAY

Cross out the letters that appear three times.

The remaining letters spell the name of a nationality.

G	R	S	K	T	O	X	B	U	V
L		G	Q	Y	A	J	Z	K	H
A	W	X	U	Z	V	D	E		M
J	P	F	L		Q	T	I	Y	G
V	S	D	I	A	B	Y	W	P	S
O	K	W	M	T	U	N	Z	L	O
D	P	J	Q	C	M	X		B	I

SPEED WORDS 4

HOW TO PLAY

Choose 10 words that fit the criteria given.

Choose words that are not proper nouns.

Use a different word for each question.

Choose a word that:		
1	Is an anagram of "MELON"	
2	Fits into "＿ E ＿ V ＿ N"	
3	Has 6 letters, and starts and ends with "W"	
4	Has 4 "S"s	
5	Has 2 "CH"s	
6	Has 4 letters and no vowels	
7	Has 9 letters and starts with "I"	
8	Has 3 syllables and starts with "Q"	
9	Rhymes with "LOOSE"	
10	Has 4 letters, and starts and ends with "C"	

WORKING IT OUT 4

HOW TO PLAY

Work out what these phrases have in common.

A pretty burgundy harmonica.

He cannot understand calculators.

We studied Japanese celebrations.

Too many aggressive alligators.

A shady clandestine operation.

X WORDS 4

HOW TO PLAY

Place the correct words in the rows in the grid so that both
diagonals spell a four-letter word reading from top to bottom.

FROM

CROW

MALL

FROM

SYNONYMS 4

HOW TO PLAY

Find the ten matching pairs of synonyms in the grid.

Rearrange the four remaining words to form a sentence

MARINER	NOVICE	YOUR	GAIETY
AROMA	WAREHOUSE	SALARY	ARMY
DAILY	PROSPERITY	SAILOR	VALET
DELUGE	TROOPS	DEPOSITORY	BEGINNER
WAGES	JOLLITY	IMPROVE	FLOOD
SERVANT	FRAGRANCE	SUCCESS	MEMORY

Sentence: _____ _____

_____ _____

FIRST AND LAST LETTERS 4

HOW TO PLAY

Think of 10 words where the first and last letters alternate.

For example, if the first word is 'REALLY', the next word would need to start with Y and end with R, the third word would then start with R and end with Y again, and so on.

Example: REALLY – YOUR – RAY – YONDER – RARITY – YEAR – RATIFY – YOUNGER – ROMANY – YOUNGSTER

Using the given words, find another 9 words with alternating first and last letters.

For words ending in S, aim to avoid using plurals.

EXIT	
SHOAL	
PIER	

SPLIT WORDS 4

HOW TO PLAY

There are eight 4-letter words that have been split into 2-letter pieces.

Find the matching parts of the eight words.

Topic: Drinks

ME	MI	WI	RT
ER	ZO	SO	BE
LA	PO	LK	CO
NE	DA	OU	AD

1. _____

2. _____

3. _____

4. _____

5. _____

6. _____

7. _____

8. _____

MEMORY GRID 4

HOW TO PLAY

Study the grid, and remember the position of the words.

Then turn the page and answer the questions.

Topic: Sports

		GOLF		
		TENNIS		
SKIING	CYCLING	BASEBALL	JAVELIN	ROWING
		SWIMMING		
		DISCUS		

MEMORY GRID 4

Questions

1. Which sport is immediately to the right of BASEBALL?

2. Which sport is directly above TENNIS?

3. Which sport is two spaces to the left of JAVELIN?

4. Which sport is directly below SWIMMING?

5. Which sport is to the immediate left of CYCLING?

6. Which sport is three spaces to the right of CYCLING?

DEFINITIONS 4

HOW TO PLAY

Choose the correct definition for each word.

Homage
A sermon
Organic constituent of soil
Dutiful reverence

Sylph
Of the woods
Slender, graceful woman
Gray crystalline rock

Cursory
Hasty, hurried
Uttering curses
Eager to learn

Pestle
Instrument for pounding
substances
Fatal epidemic disease
To annoy

Risible
Of the resurrection
Fired ball of meat with
breadcrumbs
Laughable, ludicrous

Cosmos
A substance to beautify skin
Citizen of the world
The universe as an ordered
whole

Paucity
The state of living in
poverty
Smallness of quantity
Protruding of abdomen

Quadriceps
Four-footed animal
Set of four children born at
the same time
Four-headed muscle at
front of thigh

Laconic
Brief, concise
Listless
Needy

Topiary
Reporting current affairs
Clipping shrubs into orna-
mental shapes
Aluminium silicate mineral

COLUMN WORDS 4

HOW TO PLAY

Place the words in the correct rows in the grid so that columns 2 and 5 spell out six-letter words.

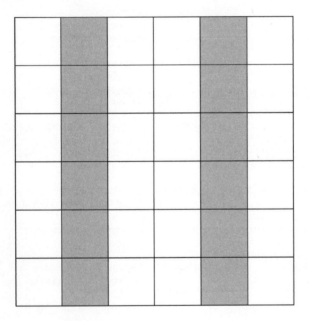

ALCOVE

STREET

EVOKED

DEPEND

TWIRLS

TENDER

STRINGS 4

HOW TO PLAY

The grid has 30 boxes.

Place words in the boxes, where the last letter of one becomes the first letter of the next. The words must fit exactly into the 30 boxes.

The theme is 'animals'. All words placed in the grid must be names of animals.

For example:

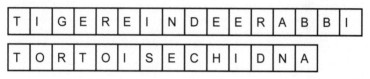

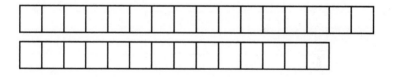

(TIGER, REINDEER, RABBIT, TORTOISE, ECHIDNA)

COMBINED ANAGRAMS 4

HOW TO PLAY

Two words have been combined and their letters arranged in alphabetical order.

Can you work out the two words?

For example the words SEVEN and EIGHT would combine to form EEEGHINSTV

Topic: Facial features

	Answer
EEHMOTUY	
BCHINORW	
CEEEHKNOS	

QUOTE GRID 4

HOW TO PLAY

Included in the grid is a one sentence quote. The words are in a continuous string, and the first word has been circled.

When you have found the quote, put the small letters from each square in the correct order into the empty grid to find a phrase relating to the quote.

G	A	T	Y	L
THINK	I	(I'VE)	THAT	COACH

M	C	M	H	O
CAN	I	IF	SAID	MY

E	S	I	P	E
DO	WELL.	FIT,	I'M	TO

WORD CAPSULE 4

HOW TO PLAY

Choose six 5-letter words that start with the letter on the left and end with the letters on the right. Choose a different word each time.

For example if the capsule was:

H				C
				L
				O
				U
				D
				Y

Your answers may be:

H	A	V	O	C
	O	V	E	L
	E	L	L	O
	A	I	K	U
	A	T	E	D
	U	R	R	Y

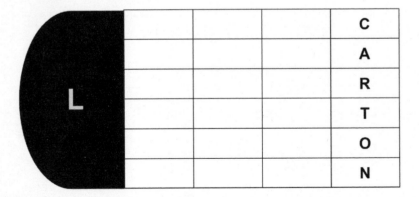

L				C
				A
				R
				T
				O
				N

MISSING ALPHABET 4

HOW TO PLAY

All 26 letters of the alphabet have been removed from this passage.

Can you put them in the correct places?

The alphabet is listed so you can cross off each letter as you place it into the passage

The tin__ man's apa__ tm__ nt __ as f__ ll of exo__ ic

items and stuf__ ed a__ imals. Hu__ e ani__ als,

su__ h as __ aguars, ele__ hant__, __ angaro__ s

an__ __ uffaloes. "Cra__ y" sa__ d M__ nuel __ uietly

to __ imse__ f, "__ ery une__ pected."

ABCDEFGHIJKLMNOPQRSTUVWXYZ

MINI WORD SUDOKU 4

HOW TO PLAY

Place the letters from the 6-letter word **RECKON** in the grid so that each column, each row, and each of the six 2×3 sub-grids contains all of the 6 letters from the word.

					C
		N			
C			E	R	
N			O		
K					O
			K		

WORDS FROM A WORD 4

HOW TO PLAY

Choose words that begin with the given letters and fit the category.

For example if the grid contained:

LETTER	CATEGORY	NUMBER OF WORDS
K	Girl's name	1
E	Occupation	2
N	Place name	3
T	Adjective	4

You would need to think of 1 girl's name beginning with K;
2 occupations beginning with; E, 3 place names beginning with N;
4 adjectives beginning with T.

LETTER	CATEGORY	NUMBER OF WORDS	WORDS
N	Part of body	On	
A	Sport	2	
P	Activity	3	
L	Adjective	4	
E	Creature	5	
S	Place name	6	

RHYMING WORDS 4

HOW TO PLAY

Find a word that rhymes with the given word and fits the definition.

For example:

WORD	DEFINITION
BARROW	Vegetable

The answer would be
MARROW

WORD	DEFINITION	RHYMING WORD
TUCKER	Aid, help	
PAID	Fabric finished with a nap	
LED	Spoken	
GUILD	Having ability	
FILE	Passage between rows	
SCROLL	Young animal	
VANE	Pretend	
HORN	Muscle	
RUNG	Not far advanced in life	
SAUCE	Husky	

NAMES 4

HOW TO PLAY

Each row has a five-letter boy's name in it with the letters rearranged, plus one extra letter.

Work out the name, then place the extra letter in the right hand column.

Rearrange the extra letters to make another name.

For example:

						Boy's name	Extra letter
E	C	F	A	L	N	LANCE	F

						Boy's name	Extra letter
A	D	S	D	V	I		
I	L	E	C	C	N		
E	D	R	K	E	T		
I	C	O	N	E	L		
I	K	E	H	T	V		
Y	L	L	D	E	O		
Additional name							

REMEMBERING NAMES AND FACES 4

There are various strategies for remembering names and faces and we will look at a number of them in these exercises.
They include:

- Repetition
    - Say the name out loud a few times
    - Write the name down a few times
- Association
    - Think about what you are most likely to remember about the person.
    - Associate the name or person with a physical characteristic e.g. rosy cheeks; someone you know; a personal characteristic e.g. smiling Linda; a famous person; a rhyming word e.g. 'Phil' and 'hill'; an item; an occupation.
    - Create a mind picture, the more unusual the better, e.g. imagine a large orange dinosaur wearing a baseball cap with the person's name on the cap

HOW TO PLAY

In this exercise, think of an emotion you could associate with the person. For example 'George looks like a kindly granddad'.

Study the people, remember the names then turn over and fill in the sheet.

| Mary | James | Jacinta |

| Robert | Isabel | Sancho |

REMEMBERING NAMES AND FACES 4

These are the six people:

CORRECTING SPELLING 4

HOW TO PLAY

Rewrite the passage, correcting any spelling mistakes.

Vernon needed too find the questionaire, and franticaly searched in the stationary cuboard.

Perserverence wasn't his strenth and he was embarased by the number of dochuments he'd recieved and missplaced.

On three seperate ocurences he'd lost clients' supoenas, though had imediatly informed his suporvisers in case they proceded to inform the perssonel departement.

He didn't want to be publiclly shamed, have his office acomodation removed and be superceded by a junior lawyer.

WORD SEARCH 4

COUNTRIES AND CAPITALS

HOW TO PLAY

The names of the countries are given and are placed in the grid vertically, horizontally or diagonally.

The capital city of these countries are also in the grid - though they are not listed - and are placed in the grid vertically, horizontally or diagonally.

Find both the country and its capital

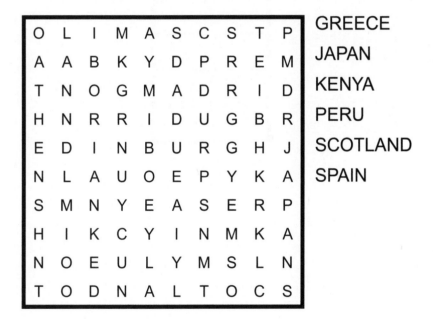

O	L	I	M	A	S	C	S	T	P
A	A	B	K	Y	D	P	R	E	M
T	N	O	G	M	A	D	R	I	D
H	N	R	R	I	D	U	G	B	R
E	D	I	N	B	U	R	G	H	J
N	L	A	U	O	E	P	Y	K	A
S	M	N	Y	E	A	S	E	R	P
H	I	K	C	Y	I	N	M	K	A
N	O	E	U	L	Y	M	S	L	N
T	O	D	N	A	L	T	O	C	S

GREECE

JAPAN

KENYA

PERU

SCOTLAND

SPAIN

WORD LADDER 4

HOW TO PLAY

Turn the first word into the last word by changing a single letter each time, making sure each step is a proper word.

WELL

FREE

CONTINUOUS WORDS 4

HOW TO PLAY

This is a list of names joined together, with the word spaces removed. How many can you find?

Topic: Capital cities

kabulalgierscanberraviennanassaubrusselssarajevogabo
ronebrasiliasofiarangoonphnompenhbeijingzagrebhava
nanicosiapraguecopenhagendjibouticairolondonaddisaba
basuvahelsinkiparistbilisiberlinaccraathensnuukgeorge
townbudapestreykjaviknewdelhijakartateheranbaghdad
dublinjerusalemromekingstontokyoammannairobiseoul
beirutmonroviatripolikualalumpurrabat

WEB WORDS 4

HOW TO PLAY

Fill in each blank square with two letters to form a six letter word with the letters diagonally above and below. The words read downwards.

For example:

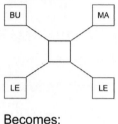

Becomes:

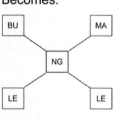

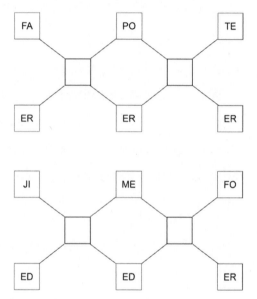

WORD CHAIN 4

HOW TO PLAY

Using one of the words, you have a minute to form a word chain by changing one letter at a time.

Repeat words are not counted.

For example, if the word were SAME, your chain might be:

FAME, TAME, TALE, TAKE, CAKE, RAKE, RAVE, RAGE, CAGE, CAVE, HAVE, GAVE, GATE, LATE, MATE, MOTE, NOTE, NOSE, ROSE, ROTE
If you come to a point where you are unable to make any more words, you can cross off the last word(s) and go back until you can continue the chain, as long as it is within the time limit.

Take a minute for each of the five words.

FEAR	
HINT	
WILY	
HERO	
CORN	

SOLVING SENTENCES 4

HOW TO PLAY

What does this sentence say?

TTH HIIS SIISSC COOR REEC CTTBB
UUTTAAL LTTH HEEL LEET TEER RSSH
HAAV VEEB BEEEE NND DOOU UBBLLE ED

TWISTER 4

HOW TO PLAY

Six words, each 6 letters long, fit into the grid, in a stepped format.

Three words go downwards and three upwards, with the middle letters being shared.

One letter is given.

If the grid and words were:

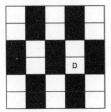

INURES, SEDATE
STADIA. STRUTS
The answer would be:

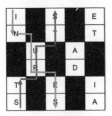

EROTIC

TRACKS

ROUTER

RETORT

CICADA

NATURE

157

TEN ADJECTIVES 4

HOW TO PLAY

Think of 10 adjectives that start with the letters given.

M	
O	
P	

FIRST LETTER 4

HOW TO PLAY

Change the first letter of each of the words in the group so that all words have the same, new, first letter. Make sure that the new words are proper words, though not proper nouns.

When you have found all the new letters, rearrange them to form a three-letter word.

	NEW LETTER
LONE - MULL - FINE - SEAT - RICE	
HARE - GORE - LACE - MILL - SEND	
CLOUD - SIDE - EWE - UMBER - SERIAL	

Word:

PATTERNS 4

HOW TO PLAY

Can you work out the pattern?

At the top of the first three columns is a name.

In the right hand column are three words that fit into the named categories.

Work out the pattern and place the words into the appropriate boxes in the grid. The first two have been done for you.

TROY	BARRY	RUSSELL	category	
BLANCA			Name of wife	COLLEEN SHEENA BLANCA
		SMALLWOOD	Surname	MATTHEWS RODRIGUEZ SMALLWOOD
			Favorite state	MASSACHUSETTS HAWAII COLORADO
			Occupa-tion	FOOTBALLER CLERK ENGINEER
			Favorite food	APPLE TOFFEE CAKE

LETTER SQUARES 4

HOW TO PLAY

Choose words that form a square going clockwise: Take the last letter of the given word, and write in a word of the same length starting with this letter and going downwards. Take the last letter of this word and write in another word starting with this letter and going to the left. Finally, take the last letter of this word and write in a word starting with this letter and ending with the first letter of the first word.

For example, if the first was SIT

You may add the words TON NOW and WAS to make

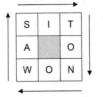

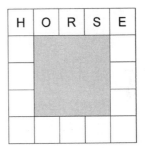

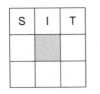

FICTIONAL LANGUAGE 4

HOW TO PLAY

A few words have been translated from English into a fictional language

Learn the translated words, then turn the page and fill in the fictional words in the gaps.

English	Fictional language
WIN	MANALOFIR
RACE	PATURUFA
GOLD	GINTOOR

FICTIONAL LANGUAGE 4
Text

Venn was nervous. Today was the athletics

competition and he was entering the 100m

_____.

He wanted to _____ and bring

home a _____ medal to

show his family and friends.

MISSING LETTERS 4

HOW TO PLAY

There are three 9-letter words that read from left to right, with the words going upwards or downwards.

Some of the letters have been taken out and are listed on the right hand side. Can you put them in the correct places?

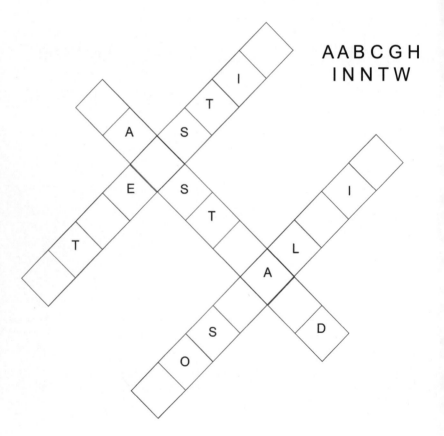

A A B C G H
I N N T W

Level 5

WORD TRAIL 5

HOW TO PLAY

Find 6 words in the grid, starting with the circled letters.

Words go vertically or horizontally.

Theme: Reptiles

D	R	A	Z	G	(I)
(P)	Y	(L)	I	U	A
H	T	A	N	A	O
O	N	E	O	N	(B)
H	(C)	L	U	(T)	E
A	M	E	R	T	L

JOINING WORDS 5

HOW TO PLAY

Find a word that completes the first word and begins the second.

The number in brackets indicates the number of letters that are missing.

SU	__ __	EM	(2)
CO	__ __	TIC	(2)
VE	__ __	EAM	(2)
JUM	__ __ __	PLEX	(3)
JAC	__ __ __	CHUP	(3)
BLO	__ __ __	FUL	(3)
SWIM	__ __ __ __	CASE	(4)
UNI	__ __ __ __	ATION	(4)
NECK	__ __ __ __	RATE	(4)

PYRAMID WORDS 5

HOW TO PLAY

Fill in the rows with words that end with the letter given.

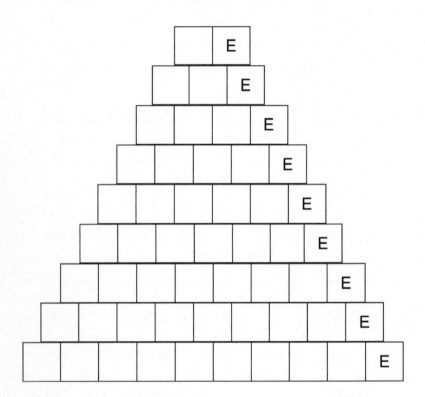

LETTER CROSS 5

HOW TO PLAY

Cross out the letters that appear three times.

The remaining letters spell the name of a part of the body.

Z	B		U	K	V	X	F	O	C
T	Q	X	J	W	Y	M	Q	Z	E
L	N	P	H		C	V	A	W	S
H	U	Z	Y	B	S	L	J	T	D
V	K	G	M	D	I	P	X	O	M
S	A	Q	J	W	D	U	K		P
C		O	L	A	T	B	H	R	Y

SPEED WORDS 5

HOW TO PLAY

Choose 10 words that fit the criteria given.

Choose words that are not proper nouns.

Use a different word for each question.

Choose a word that:		
1	Has more than 4 letters and ends in "K"	
2	Has 3 "I"s	
3	Has 2 syllables and ends in "IC"	
4	Has 4 syllables	
5	Begins with "VE" and has 3 syllables	
6	Has a "P" in the middle and has 5 or more letters	
7	Ends in "ISM"	
8	Has more than 12 letters	
9	Begins with "Z" and has more than 2 vowels	
10	Has 2 syllables that begin with the same letter	

WORKING IT OUT 5

HOW TO PLAY

Work out what is unusual about this passage.

"A kebab!" Alec said.

We—Jeff, Big Kath, I (Raj)—work well.

Jim can do group BBQ.

Clair asks Pat "Menu, luv? New gateaux—they fizz!"

X WORDS 5

HOW TO PLAY

Place the correct words in the rows in the grid so that both diagonals spell a four-letter word reading from top to bottom.

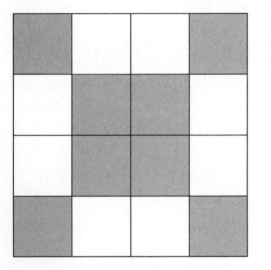

RUSE

RUNE

MANY

RIOT

SYNONYMS 5

HOW TO PLAY

Find the ten matching pairs of synonyms in the grid.

Rearrange the four remaining words to form a sentence

GIVE	MEND	BUY	SHOUT
TUG	HURT	HIT	LOCATE
FIND	IS	SMILE	GIGGLE
LAUGH	YELL	DONATE	EASY
PUNCH	PROBLEMS	INJURE	SOLVING
REPAIR	PURCHASE	PULL	GRIN

Sentence: _____ _____

_____ _____

FIRST AND LAST LETTERS 5

HOW TO PLAY

Think of 10 words where the first and last letters alternate.

For example, if the first word is "REALLY," the next word would need to start with Y and end with R, the third word would then start with R and end with Y again, and so on.

Example: REALLY – YOUR – RAY – YONDER – RARITY – YEAR – RATIFY – YOUNGER – ROMANY – YOUNGSTER

Using the given words, find another 9 words with alternating first and last letters.

For words ending in S, aim to avoid using plurals.

DIET	
NEVER	
GLASS	

SPLIT WORDS 5

HOW TO PLAY

There are five 6-letter words that have been split into 2-letter pieces.

Find the matching parts of the five words.

Topic: Countries

CE	LA	AN	EY	RD
ND	FR	RK	JO	IA
PO	SS	AN	RU	TU

1. _____

2. _____

3. _____

4. _____

5. _____

6. _____

7. _____

8. _____

MEMORY GRID 5

HOW TO PLAY

Study the grid, and remember the position of the words.

Then turn the page and answer the questions.

Topic: Parts of the body

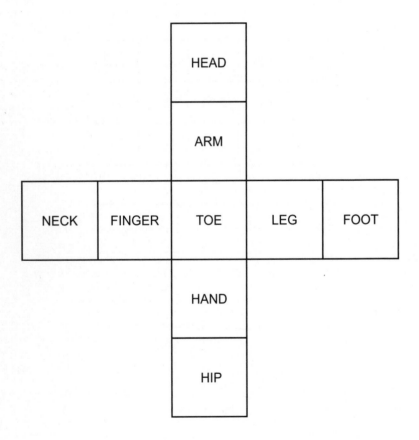

MEMORY GRID 5

Questions

1. Which part of the body is on the far right hand side?

2. Name the part of the body that is directly below the top space

3. Which part of the body is to the left of FINGER?

4. To go from ARM to TOE how many spaces down do you have to go?

5. To go from LEG to FINGER, how many spaces to the left do you have to go?

6. Name the three parts of the body that start with the letter H

DEFINITIONS 5

HOW TO PLAY

Choose the correct definition for each word.

Cacophony
- A stone coffin
- A mixture of loud and unpleasant sounds
- Pertaining to a metal wind instrument

Kerfuffle
- A piece of fabric to cover the head
- A regulation that fires be put out at a certain time
- A commotion

Fricassée
- A dish of stewed meat in a thick white sauce
- Bad tempered, difficult to control
- A noisy disturbance or quarrel

Phalanger
- A body of troops in close formation
- The practice of helping people in need
- A tree dwelling marsupial

Ruche
- A tightly packed crowd of people
- A frill or pleat of fabric
- A row or commotion

Xenophobia
- A strong dislike or fear of people from other countries
- A dry copying process
- A fear of being at the height of success

Zealot
- A person from New Zealand
- A person who follows a cause very strictly
- An inert gaseous chemical element

Attar
- A sweet selling oil made of rose petals
- A workshop or studio used by an artist
- A ring-shaped coral reef

Edifice
- The act of teaching something that is educational
- Pertaining to food that is fit to be eaten
- A large impressive building

Ignominy
- Lacking in knowledge or awareness
- Public disgrace
- Solidified molten rock

COLUMN WORDS 5

HOW TO PLAY

Place the words in the correct rows in the grid so that columns 2 and 5 spell out six-letter words.

MEMORY

ALMOST

SPRAWL

BITTER

ENTAIL

SCOUTS

STRINGS 5

HOW TO PLAY

The grid has 30 boxes.

Place words in the boxes, where the last letter of one becomes the first letter of the next. The words must fit exactly into the 30 boxes.

The theme is "girl's names." All words placed in the grid must be names of girls.

For example:

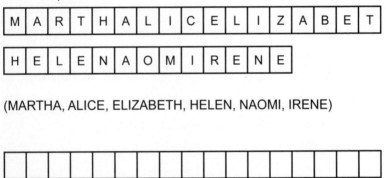

(MARTHA, ALICE, ELIZABETH, HELEN, NAOMI, IRENE)

COMBINED ANAGRAMS 5

HOW TO PLAY

Two words have been combined and their letters arranged in alphabetical order.

Can you work out the two words?

For example the words SEVEN and EIGHT would combine to form EEEGHINSTV

Topic: Sizes

	Answer
ABGILLMS	
AHLLORSTT	
AFHINTT	

QUOTE GRID 5

HOW TO PLAY

Included in the grid is a one sentence quote. The words are in a continuous string, and the first word has been circled.

When you have found the quote, put the small letters from each square in the correct order into the empty grid to find a phrase relating to the quote.

O	N	N	D	Y
FUTURE	DATE.	THE	CONSPIRACY	IN
I	**E**	**E**	**N**	**A**
A	IS	BIZARRE	MOST	THE
N	**T**	**K**	**S**	**A**
COME	AT	(IT)	HISTORY	THE
A	**I**	**S**	**S**	**S**
OUT	WILL	IT	WORLD,	OF

WORD CAPSULE 5

HOW TO PLAY

Choose six 5-letter words that start with the letter on the left and end with the letters on the right. Choose a different word each time.

For example if the capsule was:

H				C
				L
				O
				U
				D
				Y

Your answers may be:

H	A	V	O	C
	O	V	E	L
	E	L	L	O
	A	I	K	U
	A	T	E	D
	U	R	R	Y

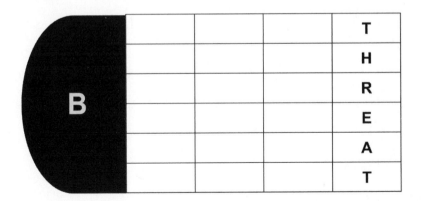

B				T
				H
				R
				E
				A
				T

MISSING ALPHABET 5

HOW TO PLAY

All 26 letters of the alphabet have been removed from this passage.

Can you put them in the correct places?

The alphabet is listed so you can cross off each letter as you place it into the passage

"I'm profes__or Far__uhar, ta__idermist . . . and

s__ightly deaf" said the __iny man.

"Woul__ y__u li__e to __oin me in wat__hin__ tele__ision?"

M__nuel __elt hesitant.

"I'm __atch__ng a docu__enta__y on gri__zl__ __ __ars.

I need to listen wit__ the so__nd tur__ed up" he

ex__lained.

ABCDEFGHIJKLMNOPQRSTUVWXYZ

MINI WORD SUDOKU 5

HOW TO PLAY

Place the letters from the 6-letter word **ENIGMA** in the grid so that each column, each row, and each of the six 2×3 sub-grids contains all of the 6 letters from the word.

		G	E		
		A		N	
			G		E
				I	
M					
	I		M		

WORDS FROM A WORD 5

HOW TO PLAY

Choose words that begin with the given letters and fit the category.

For example if the grid contained:

LETTER	CATEGORY	NUMBER OF WORDS
K	Girl's name	1
E	Occupation	2
N	Place name	3
T	Adjective	4

You would need to think of 1 girl's name beginning with K;
2 occupations beginning with; E, 3 place names beginning with N;
4 adjectives beginning with T.

LETTER	CATEGORY	NUMBER OF WORDS	WORDS
W	Tree	1	
A	Part of body	2	
R	Creature	3	
S	Food	4	
A	Occupation	5	
W	Boy's name	6	

RHYMING WORDS 5

HOW TO PLAY

Find a word that rhymes with the given word and fits the definition.

For example:

WORD	DEFINITION
BARROW	Vegetable

The answer would be
MARROW

WORD	DEFINITION	RHYMING WORD
JUICE	Conifer	
ITS	Sudden attack	
ROLE	Powder for eyelids	
SCHOOL	Net, often stiffened	
DOSE	One hundred and forty four	
TAPS	Slip of memory	
MESH	Nursery	
GATE	Cargo	
PLOT	Hit hard	
CAUGHT	Searched for	

NAMES 5

HOW TO PLAY

Each row has a five-letter girl's name in it with the letters rearranged, plus one extra letter.

Work out the name, then place the extra letter in the right hand column.

Rearrange the extra letters to make another name.

For example:

						Girl's name	Extra letter
M	A	M	E	S	G	GEMMA	S

						Girl's name	Extra letter
W	Y	E	D	J	N		
T	A	J	N	E	U		
E	L	I	K	T	Y		
E	U	L	A	A	R		
H	S	L	A	A	R		
Y	E	C	I	J	O		
Additional name							

REMEMBERING NAMES AND FACES 5

There are various strategies for remembering names and faces and we will look at a number of them in these exercises.
They include:

- Repetition
    - Say the name out loud a few times
    - Write the name down a few times
- Association
    - Think about what you are most likely to remember about the person.
    - Associate the name or person with a physical characteristic e.g. rosy cheeks; someone you know; a personal characteristic e.g. smiling Linda; a famous person; a rhyming word e.g. 'Phil' and 'hill'; an item; an occupation.
    - Create a mind picture, the more unusual the better, e.g. imagine a large orange dinosaur wearing a baseball cap with the person's name on the cap

HOW TO PLAY

In this exercise, associate the person with an occupation. The occupation and name begin with the same letter.

Study the people, remember the names then turn over and fill in the sheet.

Donald
Dentist

Amy
Accountant

Michael
Manager

Teresa
Teacher

Leroy
Librarian

Vida
Vet

REMEMBERING NAMES AND FACES 5

These are the six people:

CORRECTING SPELLING 5

HOW TO PLAY

Rewrite the passage, correcting any spelling mistakes

It had been a beatiful wedding. Susan thought Tammy looked very glamourous in her bridel gown, but being her couzin, she was undoutedly biassed. Stephen the groom looked extremelly hansome in his tucsedo, and the bridesmades wore champane-coloured dresses and permanant smiles.

They carried boquets of pastel-hued freezias. Susan tried excedingly hard not to cry as Tammy walked down the aisle and then declaired her lifelong comittment to her new husband; but most of her female relatives were trying to supress there tears. Hankerchiefs were in abundence.

The honeymoon was in the Carribean for a fourtnight in September, immediatly after the wedding.

WORD SEARCH 5

KISSING COUPLES

HOW TO PLAY

You will find the names of each couple in the shape of an X.

For example the couple DEREK and MARIE would be found:

BOBBY DEBRA
CALEB LILAC
CECIL BECKY
SHANE TRACY
VIDAL DODIE

WORD LADDER 5

HOW TO PLAY

Turn the first word into the last word by changing a single letter each time, making sure each step is a proper word.

BEEF
COWS

CONTINUOUS WORDS 5

HOW TO PLAY

This is a list of names joined together, with the word spaces removed. How many can you find?

Topic: Fruits

loganberrystrawberrydamsonmangomandarintan
gerinecherryboysenberrybananaappleguavaapricot
tamarilloorangefiggooseberrygrapefruitcantaloup
epomegranatetamarinddatepeargrapefeijoalime
blackberrymulberrypapayaavocadotomatorhubar
blycheepersimmonlemonkumquatwatermelon
kiwifruitclementinecranberrypeachplumraspberry
jackfruitcurrantpineapplequince

WEB WORDS 5

HOW TO PLAY

Fill in each blank square with two letters to form a six letter word with the letters diagonally above and below. The words read downwards.

For example:

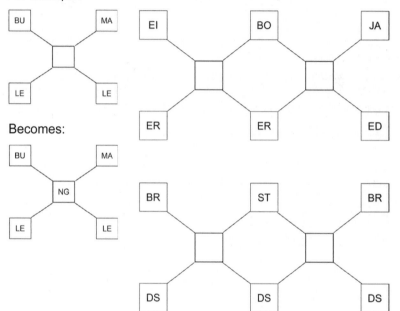

Becomes:

WORD CHAIN 5

HOW TO PLAY

Using one of the words, you have a minute to form a word chain by changing one letter at a time.

Repeat words are not counted.

For example, if the word were SAME, your chain might be:

FAME, TAME, TALE, TAKE, CAKE, RAKE, RAVE, RAGE, CAGE, CAVE, HAVE, GAVE, GATE, LATE, MATE, MOTE, NOTE, NOSE, ROSE, ROTE
If you come to a point where you are unable to make any more words, you can cross off the last word(s) and go back until you can continue the chain, as long as it is within the time limit.

Take a minute for each of the five words.

CALL	
NOTE	
NEST	
CLOG	
DEEP	

SOLVING SENTENCES 5

HOW TO PLAY

What does this sentence say?

SSD DRRA AWWKKC CAAB BSSIIEEC
CNNEET TNNEE SSEEH HTTW WOONN

TWISTER 5

HOW TO PLAY

Six words, each 6 letters long, fit into the grid, in a stepped format.

Three words go downwards and three upwards, with the middle letters being shared.

One letter is given.

If the grid and words were:

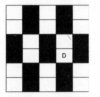

INURES, SEDATE

STADIA. STRUTS

The answer would be:

EVICTS

EDGING

STRIVE

STIGMA

DECIDE

PAIRED

TEN ADJECTIVES 5

HOW TO PLAY

Think of 10 adjectives that start with the letters given.

F	
R	
S	

FIRST LETTER 5

HOW TO PLAY

Change the first letter of each of the words in the group so that all words have the same, new, first letter. Make sure that the new words are proper words, though not proper nouns.

When you have found all the new letters, rearrange them to form a three-letter word.

	NEW LETTER
TARN - MIGHT - RYE - CAST - WIDER	
LIKE - MILL - COVER - LAND - READ	
BELL - WORE - VEST - FIRE - DUG	

Word:

PATTERNS 5

HOW TO PLAY

Can you work out the pattern?

At the top of the first three columns is a name.

In the right hand column are three words that fit into the named categories.

Work out the pattern and place the words into the appropriate boxes in the grid. The first two have been done for you.

TRACY	SALLY	MARIA	category	
			Name of husband	COLIN SHANE GERRY
	NOLAN		Surname	COREN NOLAN DRAKE
			Favorite creature	CRABS WORMS MOLES
			Favorite adjective	BORED PLAIN FALSE
		CURRY	Favorite food	BEANS CURRY MELON

LETTER SQUARES 5

HOW TO PLAY

Choose words that form a square going clockwise: Take the last letter of the given word, and write in a word of the same length starting with this letter and going downwards. Take the last letter of this word and write in another word starting with this letter and going to the left. Finally, take the last letter of this word and write in a word starting with this letter and ending with the first letter of the first word.

For example, if the first was SIT

You may add the words TON NOW and WAS to make

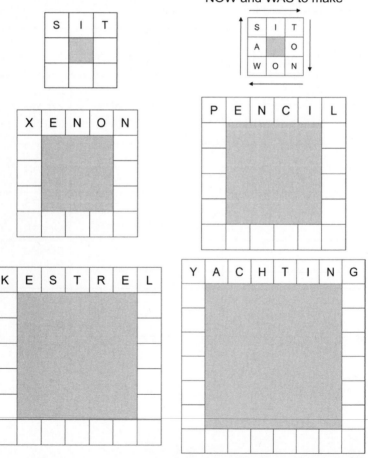

FICTIONAL LANGUAGE 5

HOW TO PLAY

A few words have been translated from English into a fictional language

Learn the translated words, then turn the page and fill in the fictional words in the gaps.

English	Fictional language
TREE	PUNOJAU
SCENTED	MABANSME
FAVORITE	PINAKITO
AZALEA	HALAMNAR

FICTIONAL LANGUAGE 5

Text

Flo loved her garden. Yellow flowers

were her _____, and she

particularly liked the beautiful laburnum

_____ .

Her prized plant was an orange

_____, followed by a sweet

_____ rose.

MISSING LETTERS 5

HOW TO PLAY

There are four 9-letter words that read from left to right, with the words going upwards or downwards.

Some of the letters have been taken out and are listed on the right hand side. Can you put them in the correct places?

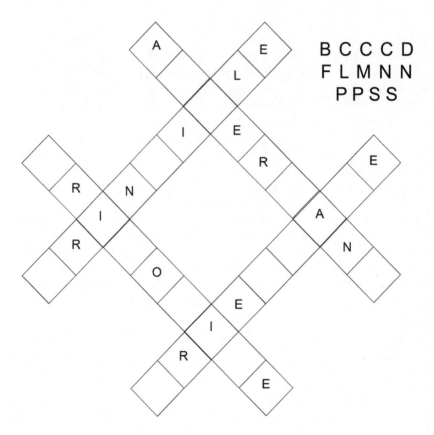

B C C C D
F L M N N
P P S S

Level 6

WORD TRAIL 6

HOW TO PLAY

Find 6 words in the grid, starting with the circled letters.

Words go vertically or horizontally.

Theme: Mammals

I	G	E	R	O	(H)
(T)	D	R	S	R	E
N	K	A	E	(L)	F
O	E	P	O	E	F
(M)	Y	B	A	R	A
T	I	B	(R)	I	(G)

JOINING WORDS 6

HOW TO PLAY

Find a word that completes the first word and begins the second.

The number in brackets indicates the number of letters that are missing.

FIN	_ _	GAE	(2)
MAN	_ _	BIT	(2)
POS	_ _	CHY	(2)
MAS	_ _ _	TAGE	(3)
NUM	_ _ _	EFT	(3)
ITA	_ _ _	ENCE	(3)
MIS	_ _ _ _	ULAR	(4)
SINE	_ _ _ _	TTE	(4)
FOOT	_ _ _ _	OLOGY	(4)

PYRAMID WORDS 6

HOW TO PLAY

Fill in the rows with words that start with the letter given.

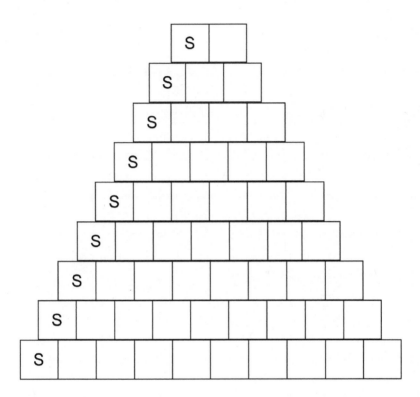

LETTER CROSS 6

HOW TO PLAY

Cross out the letters that appear three times.

The remaining letters spell the name of a type of crop

F	I	M	Q	F	Z	A	K	C	D
Q	E		Z	W		P	T	H	N
M	J	V	C	O	U	I	V	S	L
C	X	H	N	J	S	M	R	K	W
S	Y	W	X	F		D	T	G	U
G	Z	I	T	P	U	Q	V		O
J	O	N`	D	G	B	K	P	X	H

SPEED WORDS 6

HOW TO PLAY

Choose 10 words that fit the criteria given.

Choose words that are not proper nouns.

Use a different word for each question.

Choose a word that:		
1	Has 2 syllables, and starts and ends in "Y"	
2	Has 4 letters in alphabetical order	
3	Has 6 letters and ends in "C"	
4	Has 3 "G"s	
5	Has 5 letters, starts with "EE" and is not a plural	
6	Has 3 syllables and starts with "SH"	
7	Is an anagram of "ENSHOT"	
8	Fits into "P __ P __ L __ __"	
9	Has 4 syllables and starts with "H"	
10	Is a 5-letter palindrome (reads the same backwards as forwards) starting with "T"	

WORKING IT OUT 6

HOW TO PLAY

Work out what is these sentences have in common.

A "No Dog" sign! Rover barked, Natalie chuckled.

I am the only woman giving support tomorrow.

"O no," she said while Norman watched baseball.

"D. . .do you want money?" Steven shakily enquired.

X WORDS 6

HOW TO PLAY

Place the correct words in the rows in the grid so that both diagonals spell a five-letter word reading from top to bottom.

GLADE

ANODE

SINGS

SHIRT

FLOWS

Five-Minute Brain Workout

SYNONYMS 6

HOW TO PLAY

Find the ten matching pairs of synonyms in the grid.

Rearrange the four remaining words to form a sentence

SLICE	LESSEN	CUDDLE	GLEAM
GAMBLE	RETENTION	DECEIVE	DISENTANGLE
AND	PROPHESY	TREMBLE	SCARE
SHINE	EXTRICATE	FRIGHTEN	FORETELL
HUG	CUT	MEMORY	REDUCE
IMPROVE	SHAKE	BET	DUPE

Sentence: _____ _____

_____ _____

214

FIRST AND LAST LETTERS 6

HOW TO PLAY

Think of 10 words where the first and last letters alternate.

For example, if the first word is "REALLY," the next word would need to start with Y and end with R, the third word would then start with R and end with Y again, and so on.

Example: REALLY – YOUR – RAY – YONDER – RARITY – YEAR – RATIFY – YOUNGER – ROMANY – YOUNGSTER

Using the given words, find another 9 words with alternating first and last letters.

For words ending in S, aim to avoid using plurals.

HEAL	
THING	
ROAD	

SPLIT WORDS 6

HOW TO PLAY

There are five 6-letter words that have been split into 2-letter pieces.

Find the matching parts of the five words.

Topic: Animals

ET	BB	RR	NK	CO
RA	JA	DO	UG	IT
AL	AR	FE	EY	CK

1. _____

2. _____

3. _____

4. _____

5. _____

6. _____

7. _____

8. _____

MEMORY GRID 6

HOW TO PLAY

Study the grid, and remember the position of the words.

Then turn the page and answer the questions.

Topic: Nationalities

		AUSTRALIAN		
		GREEK		
ALGERIAN	POLISH	MEXICAN	JAPANESE	KENYAN
		SPANISH		
		CANADIAN		

MEMORY GRID 6

Questions

1. Which nationality is in the center of the grid?

2. Which nationality is two spaces to the left of JAPANESE?

3. Which nationality is three spaces above SPANISH?

4. Which nationality is one below and one to the right of GREEK?

5. Which nationality contains the letter D?

6. Name the two African nationalities

DEFINITIONS 6

HOW TO PLAY

Choose the correct definition for each word.

Meteoric
Philosophical state of being and knowing

Decimal measuring system

Of the atmosphere

Dorado
Blue and silver sea fish

Old, sturdy Greek style of architecture

Fictitious country abounding in gold

Knell
Large species of petrel

Hassock to kneel on

Sound of bell

Virology
Study of moral excellence

Study of viruses

Study of violence

Ylang ylang
Mythological tree whose roots and branches join heaven and earth

Malayan tree

Large African antelope

Omnivorous
Feeding on many kinds of food

Having infinite power

Being present everywhere at the same time

Gung-ho
Viscous or liquid mineral

Enthusiastic

West Indian fish

Circuitous
Being held in a public arena

The movement of blood to and from the heart

Indirect, roundabout

Leporine
Of or like hares

Suffering from leprosy

Insects with four scale-covered wings

Wraith
Anger, indignation

Twist in acute pain

Person's apparition, ghost

COLUMN WORDS 6

HOW TO PLAY

Place the words in the correct rows in the grid so that columns 2 and 5 spell out six-letter words.

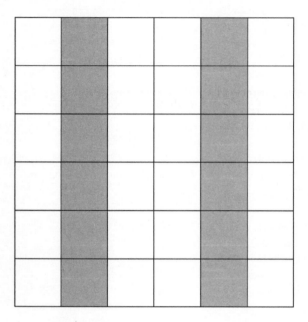

SKEWER

ASSESS

ASSIST

ACTING

PILLOW

STRUTS

STRINGS 6

HOW TO PLAY

The grid has 30 boxes.

Place words in the boxes, where the last letter of one becomes the first letter of the next. The words must fit exactly into the 30 boxes.

The theme is "boy's names." All words placed in the grid must be names of boys.

For example:

(JORDAN, NEIL, LOMAX, XAVIER, ROBERT, TIM, MARTIN)

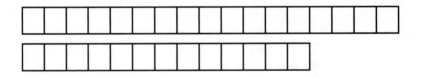

COMBINED ANAGRAMS 6

HOW TO PLAY

Two words have been combined and their letters arranged in alphabetical order.

Can you work out the two words?

For example the words SEVEN and EIGHT would combine to form EEEGHINSTV

Topic: What you can see in the sky

	Answer
MNNOOSU	
ABDEILNPR	
ACDLORSTU	

QUOTE GRID 6

HOW TO PLAY

Included in the grid is a one sentence quote. The words are in a continuous string, and the first word has been circled.

When you have found the quote, put the small letters from each square in the correct order into the empty grid to find a phrase relating to the quote.

O	M	T	A	T
DO	IS	(ALL)	AND	ONION,
T	H	B	N	U
TO	WE	PEEL	WE	AN
E	M	K	O	T
HAVE	THE	WILL	THE	LIKE
A	H	U	N	F
WITH	BE	KING	HIMSELF.	SHRINES

WORD CAPSULE 6

HOW TO PLAY

Choose six 5-letter words that start with the letter on the left and end with the letters on the right. Choose a different word each time.

For example if the capsule was:

H				C
				L
				O
				U
				D
				Y

Your answers may be:

H	A	V	O	C
	O	V	E	L
	E	L	L	O
	A	I	K	U
	A	T	E	D
	U	R	R	Y

A				S
				H
				R
				E
				W
				S

MINI WORD SUDOKU 6

HOW TO PLAY

Place the letters from the 6-letter word **PONDER** in the grid so that each column, each row, and each of the six 2×3 sub-grids contains all of the 6 letters from the word.

			O		
E				R	
	N		P		
P		O		D	
	R				N

MISSING ALPHABET 6

HOW TO PLAY

All 26 letters of the alphabet have been removed from this passage.

Can you put them in the correct places?

The alphabet is listed so you can cross off each letter as you place it into the passage

Tarquin co__ld har__ly belie__e his eyes.

The__e, in the ne__spaper w__s the m__st ama__ing

stor__ he __ad ev__r read.

__EALOUS HUS__AND CLAI__S WI__E IS IN __OVE

WI__H TAXI

"__ood gra__ious ... i__ love w__th a ta__i?" Tar__uin

as__ed him__elf, per__lexed.

ABCDEFGHIJKLMNOPQRSTUVWXYZ

WORDS FROM A WORD 6

HOW TO PLAY

Choose words that begin with the given letters and fit the category.

For example if the grid contained:

LETTER	CATEGORY	NUMBER OF WORDS
K	Girl's name	1
E	Occupation	2
N	Place name	3
T	Adjective	4

You would need to think of 1 girl's name beginning with K;
2 occupations beginning with; E, 3 place names beginning with N;
4 adjectives beginning with T.

LETTER	CATEGORY	NUMBER OF WORDS	WORDS
K	Part of body	1	
E	Country	2	
R	Sporting activity	3	
A	Adverb	4	
L	Occupation	5	
A	Creature	6	

RHYMING WORDS 6

HOW TO PLAY

Find a word that rhymes with the given word and fits the definition.

For example:

WORD	DEFINITION
BARROW	Vegetable

The answer would be
MARROW

WORD	DEFINITION	RHYMING WORD
OOZE	Injury that discolors skin	
HORDES	Rulers, chiefs, feudal superiors	
ROUSE	Large mammals	
TOES	Sleep lightly	
GAUZE	Stop temporarily	
IS	Effervesce	
SIZE	Sagacious, knowledgeable	
HE'S	Become rigid due to cold	
STAYS	North American cereal	
STOCKS	Bushy tailed animal	

NAMES 6

HOW TO PLAY

Each row has a five-letter boy's name in it with the letters rearranged, plus one extra letter.

Work out the name, then place the extra letter in the right hand column.

Rearrange the extra letters to make another name.

For example:

						Boy's name	Extra letter
E	C	F	A	L	N	LANCE	F

						Boy's name	Extra letter
R	Y	L	E	G	O		
Y	G	E	R	H	N		
V	E	N	I	K	R		
M	O	O	I	N	S		
E	J	S	A	E	M		
E	K	C	C	H	U		
Additional name							

REMEMBERING NAMES AND FACES 6

There are various strategies for remembering names and faces and we
will look at a number of them in these exercises.
They include:
- Repetition
    - Say the name out loud a few times
    - Write the name down a few times
- Association
    - Think about what you are most likely to remember about the
      person
    - Associate the name or person with a physical characteristic
      e.g. rosy cheeks; someone you know; a personal characteristic
      e.g. smiling Linda; a famous person; a rhyming word e.g. 'Phil'
      and 'hill'; an item; an occupation
    - Create a mind picture, the more unusual the better, e.g.
      imagine a large orange dinosaur wearing a baseball cap with
      the person's name on the cap

HOW TO PLAY

In this exercise, associate the person with their facial expression

Study the people, remember the names then turn over and fill in the sheet.

Rebecca
Surprised

Bobby
Kindly

Carolyn
Perplexed

Louis
Laughing

Amanda
Annoyed

Jeremy
Calm

REMEMBERING NAMES AND FACES 6

These are the six people:

CORRECTING SPELLING 6

HOW TO PLAY

Rewrite the passage, correcting any spelling mistakes.

Johnny was four years old and his mother and father ocassionally made an exeption to his 7p.m. bedtime routeine.

This time they alowed him to stay up late to watch the openning ceromony of the Olympics as it promissed to be a memorible ocassion.

He was fasinated and watched with grate intrest, often interupting to ask pertinant questions.

His mother explianed that at the subsecquent the Olympics he would be eight years old.

Later, they where all feelling exhausted, and went to bed. The folowing morning Johnny's parents where looking at the Olympic sports shedule: decathalon, fenceing, canoing . . .

Johnny looked at the telivision, obzerving that the Olympics where on again.

Astonnished, he turned to his mother and enquiered "Am I eight now?"

WORDSEARCH 6
DOWNWORDS

HOW TO PLAY

There are 10 words starting on the top line and working their way down in a continuous string to the bottom, either vertically or diagonally.

For example the word FUNDRAISER would be found:

S	S	S	S	S	S	S	S	S	S
C	A	H	E	K	I	L	P	O	T
A	O	C	I	A	U	L	E	L	R
N	R	C	M	L	H	M	I	C	E
O	D	S	K	O	L	C	B	N	I
A	S	T	I	F	U	I	E	G	A
L	A	R	N	E	U	R	T	L	T
I	N	E	G	T	I	L	I	O	H
C	Z	L	S	N	T	L	S	E	U
E	T	S	Y	E	G	T	Y	N	S

SACROSANCT
SCANDALIZE
SEAMSTRESS
SHOCKINGLY
SILHOUETTE
SKILLFULLY
SLUMBERING
SOLICITOUS
SPECIALIST
STRENGTHEN

WORD LADDER 6

HOW TO PLAY

Turn the first word into the last word by changing a single letter each time, making sure each step is a proper word.

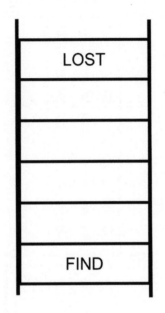

CONTINUOUS WORDS 6

HOW TO PLAY

This is a list of names joined together, with the word spaces removed. How many can you find?

Topic: Colors

shockingpinkkhakiivoryyellowwhiteecruultrama
rineemeraldjadeamberrusttaupecerisescarletteallave
nderredburgundyamethystnavyvioletburntorangeapri
cotmustardmagentaaquamarinegreenmidnightblueau
burnazurebeigegoldindigoorangeolivemauvebluepea
chcharcoallilaccinnamonbrownbronzecreamcrimson
maroonmagnoliacyanfuchsiasalmonpurplepleperiwinkle

WEB WORDS 6

HOW TO PLAY

Fill in each blank square with two letters to form a six letter word with the letters diagonally above and below. The words read downwards.

For example:

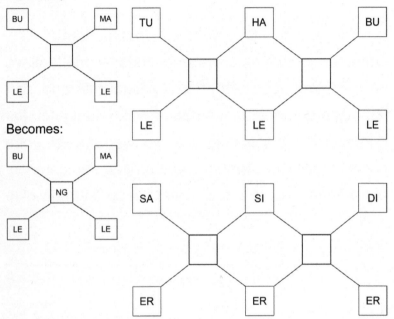

Becomes:

WORD CHAIN 6

HOW TO PLAY

Using one of the words, you have a minute to form a word chain by changing one letter at a time.

Repeat words are not counted.

For example, if the word were

SAME, your chain might be:

FAME, TAME, TALE, TAKE, CAKE, RAKE, RAVE, RAGE, CAGE, CAVE, HAVE, GAVE, GATE, LATE, MATE, MOTE, NOTE, NOSE,, ROSE, ROTE

If you come to a point where you are unable to make any more words, you can cross off the last word(s) and go back until you can continue the chain, as long as it is within the time limit.

Take a minute for each of the five words.

HOPE	
RISE	
LAZY	
BACK	
CREW	

SOLVING SENTENCES 6

HOW TO PLAY

What do these sentences say?

SAME AS ESKIMO VERB RIDGE.

HEAR RANGE DEAR LIE RE VENTS.

TO MATE TENT ART SAND AS A LAD.

TWISTER 6

HOW TO PLAY

Six words, each 6 letters long, fit into the grid, in a stepped format.

Three words go downwards and three upwards, with the middle letters being shared.

One letter is given.

If the grid and words were:

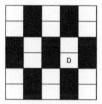

INURES, SEDATE

STADIA. STRUTS

The answer would be:

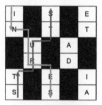

EVINCE

REREAD

COOLER

DANISH

ALLOWS

SWERVE

239

TEN ADJECTIVES 6

HOW TO PLAY

Think of 10 adjectives that start with the letters given.

D	
I	
N	

FIRST LETTER 6

HOW TO PLAY

Change the first letter of each of the words in the group so that all words have the same, new, first letter. Make sure that the new words are proper words, though not proper nouns.

When you have found all the new letters, rearrange them to form a three-letter word.

	NEW LETTER
WASTE - BINGE - POOL - FRIES - VEND	
TOUCH - MERGER - LOW - EASE - SOLE	
SLOPE - SQUALLY - RATING - CASE - GLIDE	

Word:

PATTERNS 6

HOW TO PLAY

Can you work out the pattern?

At the top of the first three columns is a name.

In the right hand column are three words that fit into the named categories.

Work out the pattern and place the words into the appropriate boxes in the grid. The first two have been done for you.

LYNN	ANN	JEAN	category	
			Name of husband	GLYN NEIL JOHN
	BURNS		Surname	BURNS CLOUGH MᶜFLY
			Occupation	CLERK GYPSY COACH
			Favorite activity	SQUASH CHESS GYM
		DEER	Favorite animal	DEER LYNX PIG

LETTER SQUARES 6

HOW TO PLAY

Choose words that form a square going clockwise: Take the last letter of the given word, and write in a word of the same length starting with this letter and going downwards. Take the last letter of this word and write in another word starting with this letter and going to the left. Finally, take the last letter of this word and write in a word starting with this letter and ending with the first letter of the first word.

For example, if the first was SIT

You may add the words TON NOW and WAS to make

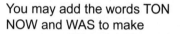

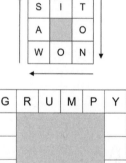

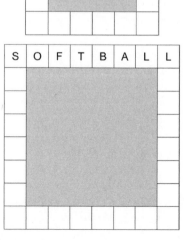

FICTIONAL LANGUAGE 6

HOW TO PLAY

A few words have been translated from English into a fictional language

Learn the translated words, then turn the page and fill in the fictional words in the gaps.

English	Fictional language
ASKED	NAGTANQUE
FIVE	LIMAQUI
QUESTIONS	TANONDOX
SKY	LANGITIEL

FICTIONAL LANGUAGE 6
Text

Her son was _____

years old and loved posing challenging

_____ .

"Mommy" he said "do stars fall out of the

_____ and into the sea?"

"No," she replied, "why?"

"Well where do starfish come from

then?" he _____.

Level 7

WORD TRAIL 7

HOW TO PLAY

Find 6 words in the grid.

Words go vertically or horizontally.

Theme: Composers

D	N	A	H	M	S
E	K	H	A	L	E
L	A	R	R	G	A
D	E	O	B	C	R
U	B	V	D	H	O
S	S	Y	N	I	P

JOINING WORDS 7

HOW TO PLAY

Find a word that completes the first word and begins the second.

The number in brackets indicates the number of letters that are missing.

WHA	— —	VER	(2)
LI	— —	CE	(2)
FR	— —	RE	(2)
WAL	— — —	SET	(3)
CH	— — —	ALE	(3)
CA	— — —	ODY	(3)
LEO	— — — —	ON	(4)
FLAM	— — — —	T	(4)
WAL	— — — —	RINTH	(4)

PYRAMID WORDS 7

HOW TO PLAY

Fill in the rows with words that end with the letter given.

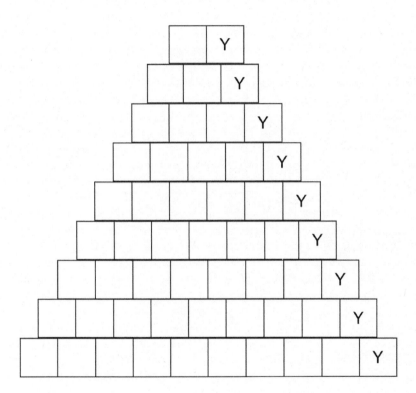

LETTER CROSS 7

HOW TO PLAY

Cross out the letters that appear four times.

The remaining letters spell the name of a color.

D	Z	N	K	G		C	U	I	M
P	O	A	S	D	X	J	R	B	W
U	G	Q	M	Y	B	Z	F		P
K	W	Z	C	U	Z	N	W	V	J
A	S	F	Y	H	Q	X	D	H	X
R		Q	A	N	D	J	G	C	R
F	J	B	E	R	T	Y	B	U	K
L	M	P	S	G		M	P	H	S
N	C	H	F	Q	K	W	A	X	Y

SPEED WORDS 7

HOW TO PLAY

Choose 10 words that fit the criteria given.

Choose words that are not proper nouns.

Use a different word for each question.

Choose a word that:		
1	Rhymes with "ORDER"	
2	Has 2 syllables where both syllables rhyme with "who"	
3	Has 6 letters and no vowels	
4	Is an anagram of 2 words combined, "LAY" and "SAW"	
5	Has 2 "Z"s and one "Q"	
6	Has 6 letters, starts with "Z" and isn't a plural	
7	Has 4 syllables and starts with "M"	
8	Has 6 letters, including 3 "E"s	
9	Fits into "__ I __ I __ __ __"	
10	Has 12 letters and starts with "A"	

WORKING IT OUT 7

HOW TO PLAY

Work out what is unusual about this passage.

"Hi, I'll call Mike," Gail claimed.

Jade called, "He emailed me."

"I'm glad Jade. I like him; he made me feel laidback."

"Hmmm, Liam claimed he blackmailed him."

"Aah, Liam did, did he? I'll call him."

X WORDS 7

HOW TO PLAY

Place the correct words in the rows in the grid so that both diagonals spell a five-letter word reading from top to bottom.

TRUST

FLAKE

WATER

SPINS

SYNONYMS 7

HOW TO PLAY

Find the twelve matching pairs of synonyms in the grid.

Rearrange the four remaining words to form a sentence

YEARLY	PERMIT	MIDDLE	ARE
EDUCATIONAL	EMPTY	BUSY	OFTEN
ANCIENT	DETEST	ORAL	CHAMPION
START	PUZZLES	CONFESS	BEGIN
WINNER	BLANK	ALLOW	WORD
ADMIT	VERBAL	ANNUAL	HATE
ACTIVE	CENTER	FREQUENTLY	OLD

Sentence: _____ _____

_____ _____

FIRST AND LAST LETTERS 7

HOW TO PLAY

Think of 10 words where the first and last letters alternate.

For example, if the first word is "REALLY," the next word would need to start with Y and end with R, the third word would then start with R and end with Y again, and so on.

Example: REALLY – YOUR – RAY – YONDER – RARITY – YEAR – RATIFY – YOUNGER – ROMANY – YOUNGSTER

Using the given words, find another 9 words with alternating first and last letters.

For words ending in S, aim to avoid using plurals.

LAST	
DRESS	
HEAR	

SPLIT WORDS 7

HOW TO PLAY

There are five 6-letter words that have been split into 2-letter pieces.

Find the matching parts of the five words.

Topic: Cities

NI	LO	ES	ON	GE
NO	NE	BE	VE	RL
IN	CE	ND	VA	FR

1. _____

2. _____

3. _____

4. _____

5. _____

MEMORY GRID 7

HOW TO PLAY

Study the grid, and remember the position of the words.

Then turn the page and answer the questions.

Topic: Adjectives

		PATIENT		
		HAPPY		
ANIMATED	LIVELY	CALM	DYNAMIC	EXCITING
		PLEASANT		
		CARING		

MEMORY GRID 7

Questions

1. Which adjectives are at the top and the bottom?

2. Which adjectives are on the far left and the far right?

3. Which adjective is to the immediate right of CALM?

4. Which adjectives end in the letter Y?

5. Which adjective is directly above CARING?

6. Which adjective is two spaces to the left and two spaces up from EXCITING?

DEFINITIONS 7

HOW TO PLAY

Choose the correct definition for each word.

Clandestine
Truthful and straight-forward
Expressing sympathy
Kept secret

Feverfew
State of nervous excitement
Plant with daisy-like flowers
Healthy, rarely ill

Beatitude
The act of making beautiful
Very great happiness or blessedness
Having no justifiable reason

Expatiate
Speak or write at great length about
A person who lives outside their native country
To send someone back to their own country

Zephyr
A spirit in nature in the form of a young woman
A small imaginary being with magical powers
A soft gentle breeze

Obdurate
Unpleasant or offensive
Stubbornly refusing to change ones mind
Respectful, willing to comply

Plangent
Loud and mournful
Tiny organisms living in the sea
English royal dynasty

Radicchio
Variety of chicory with dark red leaves
Part of plant that develops into a primary root
Plucking the strings of a musical instrument with your fingers

Uvula
To howl or wail
A person who takes over someone's position by force
Fleshy part of soft palate that hangs above the throat

Saithe
An X-shaped cross
An edible North Atlantic fish
To wrap in several layers of fabric

COLUMN WORDS 7

HOW TO PLAY

Place the words in the correct rows in the grid so that columns 2 and 5 spell out sixletter words.

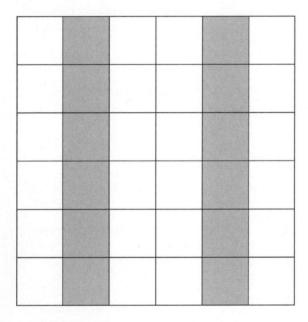

FLOWER

TENORS

TENNIS

IMPOSE

AFRESH

PALATE

STRINGS 7

HOW TO PLAY

The grid has 30 boxes.

Place words in the boxes, where the last letter of one becomes the first letter of the next. The words must fit exactly into the 30 boxes.

The theme is 'food'. All words placed in the grid must be names of types of food.

For example:

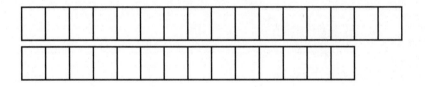

S	T	R	A	W	B	E	R	R	Y	A	M	U	S	H	R

O	O	M	A	N	G	O	R	A	N	G	E	G	G

(STRAWBERRY, YAM, MUSHROOM, MANGO, ORANGE, EGG)

COMBINED ANAGRAMS 7

HOW TO PLAY

Two words have been combined and their letters arranged in alphabetical order.

Can you work out the two words?

For example the words SEVEN and EIGHT would combine to form EEEGHINSTV

Topic: Food

	Answer
AHKMOPR	
AABDENRTU	
BCEEEEEFHS	
ACCEIORRRT	

QUOTE GRID 7

HOW TO PLAY

Included in the grid is a one sentence quote. The words are in a continuous string, and the first word has been circled.

When you have found the quote, put the small letters from each square in the correct order into the empty grid to find a phrase relating to the quote.

YEARS ^E	THE ^R	POLITICIANS. ^N	ITS ^O	IN ^I
(EVERY) ^A	TWO ^M	AMERICAN ^I		TRUST ^T
INDUSTRY ^A	POLITICS ^C	DECLARES ^L	AMERICA ^L	LOST ^C
FILLS ^N		THAT ^E	THEN ^A	HAS ^E
AIRWAVES ^R	THE ^P	ASSASSINA-TIONS ^I	OF ^D	AND ^I
WITH ^E	CHARACTER ^S	EVERY ^E	POLITICAL ^N	PRACTITIONER ^T

WORD CAPSULE 7

HOW TO PLAY

Choose six 5-letter words that start with the letter on the left and end with the letters on the right. Choose a different word each time.

For example if the capsule was:

H				C
				L
				O
				U
				D
				Y

Your answers may be:

H	A	V	O	C
	O	V	E	L
	E	L	L	O
	A	I	K	U
	A	T	E	D
	U	R	R	Y

D				S
				T
				R
				O
				N
				G

MISSING ALPHABET 7

HOW TO PLAY

All 26 letters of the alphabet have been removed from this passage.

Can you put them in the correct places?

The alphabet is listed so you can cross off each letter as you place it into the passage

The man's __ife was w__th her __eloved taxi

__ll da__ l__ng.

S__e clea__ed, wa__ed and __olished it

lo__ingly, n__ve__ __ ues__ioning how stran__e

it see__e__ .

__he __ailed to reali__e how re__ected it

__o__ld ma__e a man fee__

ABCDEFGHIJKLMNOPQRSTUVWXYZ

MINI WORD SUDOKU 7

HOW TO PLAY

Place the letters from the 6-letter word **NUMBER** in the grid so that each column, each row, and each of the six 2×3 sub-grids contains all of the 6 letters from the word.

M					
		N	R		M
	E			R	
	N		M	U	
N		U			
	M				U

WORDS FROM A WORD 7

HOW TO PLAY

Choose words that begin with the given letters and fit the category.

For example if the grid contained:

LETTER	CATEGORY	NUMBER OF WORDS
K	Girl's name	1
E	Occupation	2
N	Place name	3
T	Adjective	4

You would need to think of 1 girl's name beginning with K;
2 occupations beginning with; E, 3 place names beginning with N;
4 djectives beginning with T.

LETTER	CATEGORY	NUMBER OF WORDS	WORDS
M	Language	1	
O	Bird	2	
S	Color	3	
C	Part of body	4	
O	Place name	5	
W	Action verb	6	

RHYMING WORDS 7

HOW TO PLAY

Find a word that rhymes with the given word and fits the definition.

For example:

WORD	DEFINITION
BARROW	Vegetable

The answer would be
MARROW

WORD	DEFINITION	RHYMING WORD
FROZE	Fragrant flower	
THESE	Exert pressure on	
RAISE	To look intently at	
BOX	Appliances for fastening items	
SIX	Shoots of a tree cut to length	
SPECKS	To bend	
SLACKS	Chopping tool	
YOU'VE	To change position of	
SIEVE	To transfer possession of	
GRIEVE	The day before	

NAMES 7

HOW TO PLAY

Each row has a five-letter boy's name in it with the letters rearranged, plus one extra letter.

Work out the name, then place the extra letter in the right hand column.

Rearrange the extra letters to make another name.

For example:

						Boy's name	Extra letter
E	C	F	A	L	N	LANCE	F

						Boy's name	Extra letter
Y	A	B	B	B	O		
O	S	N	A	T	J		
I	R	B	A	R	N		
L	L	N	Y	N	E		
N	E	G	R	T	A		
E	W	O	D	I	G		
Additional name							

REMEMBERING NAMES AND FACES 7

There are various strategies for remembering names and faces and we will look at a number of them in these exercises.
They include:

- Repetition
    - Say the name out loud a few times
    - Write the name down a few times
- Association
    - Think about what you are most likely to remember about the person.
    - Associate the name or person with a physical characteristic e.g. rosy cheeks; someone you know; a personal characteristic e.g. smiling Linda; a famous person; a rhyming word e.g. 'Phil' and 'hill'; an item; an occupation.
    - Create a mind picture, the more unusual the better, e.g. imagine a large orange dinosaur wearing a baseball cap with the person's name on the cap

HOW TO PLAY

In this exercise, create a mind picture for each person, the stranger the better.

Study the people, remember the names then turn over and fill in the sheet.

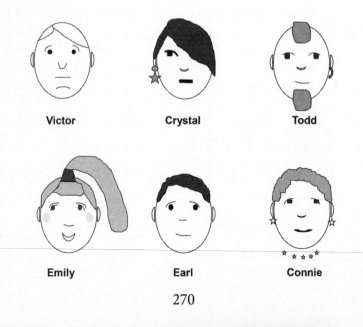

| Victor | Crystal | Todd |
| Emily | Earl | Connie |

REMEMBERING NAMES AND FACES 7

These are the six people:

CORRECTING SPELLING 7

HOW TO PLAY

Rewrite the passage, correcting any spelling mistakes.

Gregory Harris was haveing a challengeing day. Bieng principle of a kindergarden was a prestigous role, but a busy one.

Sometimes he had to teach, whitch meant he had to constantly develope his knowlege. This week he gave lessens on squirells, ostridges, and penguins, and helped with rehersals for the upcomeing show.

He wonderd about the feasability of emplying anouther teacher but the figures simpley didn't add up. They're weren't suficient funds.

"Money, we allways need money," he said to himself forelornly.

"Mr Harris," said a conserned four-year-old, "woud you like some of my pockit money?"

WORDSEARCH 7

TWO FOUR SIX EIGHT

HOW TO PLAY

The words TWO, FOUR, SIX, EIGHT are placed in the grid:

TWO is there twice

FOUR is there four times

SIX is there six times

EIGHT is there eight times

U	F	H	E	F	S	H	E	E	X
E	E	S	W	I	R	W	I	U	I
H	I	S	X	U	G	G	G	W	S
X	G	G	O	F	H	H	H	R	S
R	H	F	H	T	V	W	T	U	S
U	T	S	O	T	U	H	S	O	I
O	H	U	W	F	G	W	V	F	X
F	G	V	T	I	X	R	U	O	F
S	I	X	E	I	F	T	W	O	U
F	E	H	S	R	T	H	G	I	E

TWO X 2

FOUR X 4

SIX X 6

EIGHT X 8

WORD LADDER 7

HOW TO PLAY

Turn the first word into the last word by changing a single letter each time, making sure each step is a proper word.

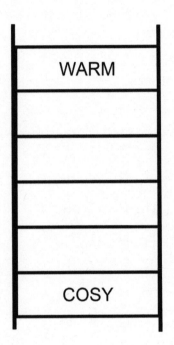

CONTINUOUS WORDS 7

HOW TO PLAY

This is a list of names joined together, with the word spaces removed. How many can you find?

Topic: Items that are green

grasshopperkiwifruitturtleeyesshamrockkelppar
sleyzucchiniiguanaalgaeelvessnakeemeraldgr
apeperidotlettucecressspinachhollykryptonitef
ernmoneylizardbroccolijadeavocadoolivecelery
grassspirulinaapplepeassproutschrysaliscaterp
illarpepperclovercactusmossmintlimeartichokec
ucumbermarrowfrogcabbageasparaguslea
fprayingmantis

WEB WORDS 7

HOW TO PLAY

Fill in each blank square with two letters to form a six letter word
with the letters diagonally above and below. The words read
downwards.

For example

Becomes:

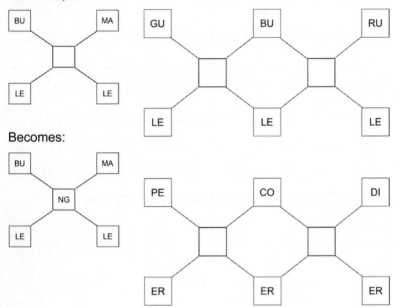

WORD CHAIN 7

HOW TO PLAY

Using one of the words, you have a minute to form a word chain by changing one letter at a time.

Repeat words are not counted.

For example, if the word were SAME, your chain might be:

FAME, TAME, TALE, TAKE, CAKE, RAKE, RAVE, RAGE, CAGE, CAVE, HAVE, GAVE, GATE, LATE, MATE, MOTE, NOTE, NOSE, ROSE, ROTE

If you come to a point where you are unable to make any more words, you can cross off the last word(s) and go back until you can continue the chain, as long as it is within the time limit.

Take a minute for each of the five words.

MESH	
DRAG	
SNOW	
FLEE	
WORK	

SOLVING SENTENCES 7

HOW TO PLAY

What do these sentences say?

MERET YOURUR TERAM NERIL.
AVORID THERIR LORUD NORISY
FERUD THORUGH, IRT WERARS URS
ORUT

TWISTER 7

HOW TO PLAY

Six words, each 6 letters long, fit into the grid, in a stepped format.

Three words go downwards and three upwards, with the middle letters being shared.

One letter is given.

If the grid and words were:

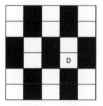

INURES, SEDATE
STADIA. STRUTS

The answer would be:

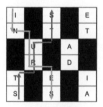

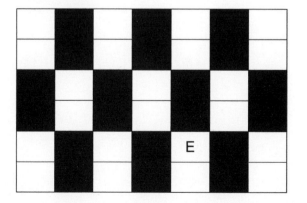

SEETHE

SPARED

DENIAL

SCRAPS

LATENT

SPINES

TEN ADJECTIVES 7

HOW TO PLAY

Think of 10 adjectives that start with the letters given.

A	
E	
W	

FIRST LETTER 7

HOW TO PLAY

Change the first letter of each of the words in the group so that all words have the same, new, first letter. Make sure that the new words are proper words, though not proper nouns.

When you have found all the new letters, rearrange them to form a threeletter word.

	NEW LETTER
SPRIGHT - ONION - KNIT - AMBER - INTO	
AIM - MINE - PRESS - OUNCE - SHOW	
FEAT - LINK - CORE - RUST - DARE	

Word:

PATTERNS 7

HOW TO PLAY

Can you work out the pattern?

At the top of the first three columns is a name.

In the right hand column are three words that fit into the named categories.

Work out the pattern and place the words into the appropriate boxes in the grid. The first two have been done for you.

SEAN	MIKE	PHIL	category	
			Name of wife	KATE JOAN NELL
BROWN			Favorite color	TEAL WHITE BROWN
	POODLE		Favorite dog	DALMATION SPANIEL POODLE
			Favorite superhero	HAWKEYE HAWKMAN HAWKGIRL
			Favorite flower	BLUEBELL ANEMONE CYCLAMEN

LETTER SQUARES 7

HOW TO PLAY

Choose words that form a square going clockwise: Take the last letter of the given word, and write in a word of the same length starting with this letter and going downwards. Take the last letter of this word and write in another word starting with this letter and going to the left. Finally, take the last letter of this word and write in a word starting with this letter and ending with the first letter of the first word.

For example, if the first was SIT

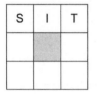

You may add the words TON NOW and WAS to make

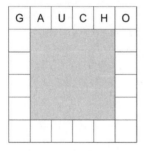

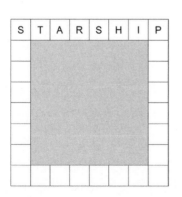

283

FICTIONAL LANGUAGE 7

HOW TO PLAY

A few words have been translated from English into a fictional language

Learn the translated words, then turn the page and fill in the fictional words in the gaps.

English	Fictional language
LUMPY	BUKOLUN
OPEN	BUKASAB
ROOM	KUWARSAL
TOAST	TUSTAGRIL

FICTIONAL LANGUAGE 7
Text

It was the worst holiday they had ever been on!

The hotel _____ was dirty, the mattresses were _____ and the windows wouldn't _____.

The hotel staff who made breakfast even managed to burn the _____.

Level 8

WORD TRAIL 8

HOW TO PLAY

Find 6 words in the grid.

Words go vertically or horizontally.

Theme: Vegetables

A	R	R	O	S	P
C	T	E	T	O	R
R	U	G	T	U	N
N	B	A	P	U	R
I	B	A	C	M	O
P	N	I	K	P	C

JOINING WORDS 8

HOW TO PLAY

Find a word that completes the first word and begins the second.

The number in brackets indicates the number of letters that are missing.

PLACA	__ __	NSION	(2)
LIV	__ __	ENTIFY	(2)
TANGR	__ __	POULE	(2)
ANAE	__ __ __	ROBE	(3)
MID	__ __ __	SIDE	(3)
TANK	__ __ __	UOUS	(3)
FE	__ __ __ __	VOLENT	(4)
HO	__ __ __ __	LAR	(4)
NAR	__ __ __ __	PAYER	(4)

PYRAMID WORDS 8

HOW TO PLAY

Fill in the rows with words that end with the letter given.

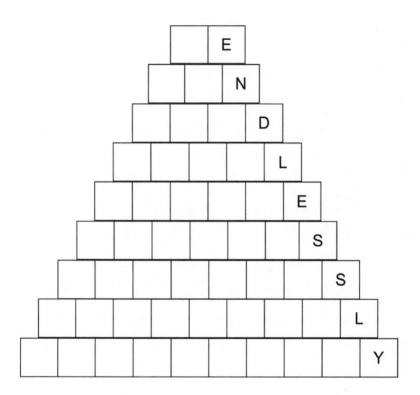

LETTER CROSS 8

HOW TO PLAY

Cross out the letters that appear four times.

The remaining letters spell the name of a marine mammal.

G	X	N	V	C	V	N	K	R	Q
Y	L	C	E	I	G	W	H		F
J	Z	Y	H	F	B	Y	D	P	O
P	T	D	X	M	K	T	N	G	Z
G		Z	Q	P	V	X	B	J	E
B	F	A	T	E	H	D	I		X
O	K	Y	M	J	Z	N	P	C	J
Q	E	O		S	I	O	U	K	V
B	I	T	F	M	Q	C	H	M	D

SPEED WORDS 8

HOW TO PLAY

Choose 10 words that fit the criteria given.

Choose words that are not proper nouns.

Use a different word for each question.

Choose a word that:		
1	Has 5 syllables	
2	Is a palindrome (reads the same forwards and backwards), longer than 5 letters	
3	Rhymes with "BREATHE"	
4	Begins with "HY" and has more than 3 syllables	
5	Begins and ends with the same 2 letters and is longer than 5 letters	
6	Has 7 letters. The middle letter is "S"	
7	Has the letters "KH" together in the body of the word	
8	Has 2 "T"s and 2 "S"s	
9	Has 5 letters in alphabetical order	
10	Has 7 letters but only 1 syllable	

WORKING IT OUT 8

HOW TO PLAY

Work out what is unusual about this passage.

"Aha," said Hannah, "the stats are level.

The racecar, not kayak, is redder.

The tenet is: solos have sagas.

Sir Bob was deified at Glenelg, and Eve will refer to Madam Smith, civic dignitary."

X WORDS 8

HOW TO PLAY

Place the correct words in the rows in the grid so that both diagonals spell a five-letter word reading from top to bottom.

SPADE

SWIMS

COURT

FOLIC

PLOYS

SYNONYMS 8

HOW TO PLAY

Find the twelve matching pairs of synonyms in the grid.

Rearrange the four remaining words to form a sentence

VISIBLE	ENDED	JUSTIFIABLE	CONCISE
BENEFICIAL	SULKY	WATCHFUL	EXTRA
BRIEF	STERN	YOUR	USEFUL
DAILY	FRUGAL	CONSPICUOUS	FAULTLESS
ADDITIONAL	ALERT	DO	WEIGHTY
HEAVY	DEFENSIBLE	MOROSE	AUSTERE
TRAINING	TERMINATED	IMMACULATE	MISERLY

Sentence: _____ _____

_____ _____

FIRST AND LAST LETTERS 8

HOW TO PLAY

Think of 10 words where the first and last letters alternate.

For example, if the first word is "REALLY," the next word would need to start with Y and end with R, the third word would then start with R and end with Y again, and so on.

Example: REALLY – YOUR –
RAY – YONDER – RARITY – YEAR – RATIFY – YOUNGER –
ROMANY – YOUNGSTER

Using the given words, find another 9 words with alternating first and last letters.

For words ending in S, aim to avoid using plurals.

GOAL	
RIOT	
DEVIL	

SPLIT WORDS 8

HOW TO PLAY

There are five 6-letter words that have been split into 2-letter pieces.

Find the matching parts of the five words.

Topic: Colors

OL	YE	RP	LV	LL
PU	VI	SI	OW	MA
ER	ON	ET	RO	LE

1. _____

2. _____

3. _____

4. _____

5. _____

MEMORY GRID 8

HOW TO PLAY

Study the grid, and remember the position of the words.

Then turn the page and answer the questions.

Topic: Types of building

		CASTLE		
		GALLERY		
CABIN	GARAGE	STORE	HOUSE	THEATER
		TEMPLE		
		PALACE		

MEMORY GRID 8

Questions

1. Which type of building is immediately to the left of the center space?

2. Which type of building is four spaces below CASTLE?

3. Which types of building have seven letters?

4. In relation to the center space, where is TEMPLE?

5. Which type of building is three spaces to the left of HOUSE?

6. How many types of building end in the letter E?

DEFINITIONS 8

HOW TO PLAY

Choose the correct definition for each word.

Privation
Loss or absence
Right, advantage or immunity
Army vessel

Thither
Prickly herbaceous plant
To that place
Flat, many-stringed instrument

Ingurgitate
Swallow greedily
Start of eclipse
Bring oneself into favour with

Desalinate
Regret absence of
To devastate
Remove salt from

Noggin
Trifling, worthless
Small mug or measure
Small peg made of wood

Hoopoe
Game played with wooden board and hoops
Bird with variegated plumage
To play truant

Scilla
Bulbous plant
Greek Mythological monster
Eyelash

Vintner
Of high quality from the past
Grape-gatherer
Wine merchant

Ambiversion
Double meaning
Holding opposite emotional attitudes
Balance between introversion and extroversion

Kanaka
Member of Dravidian people living in India
Pacific islander
Follower of the Hindu god of love

COLUMN WORDS 8

HOW TO PLAY

Place the words in the correct rows in the grid so that columns 2 and 5 spell out
six-letter words.

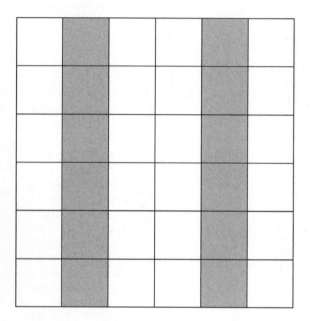

MAJORS

ADRIFT

RHYTHM

ASPECT

DINING

ANSWER

STRINGS 8

HOW TO PLAY

The grid has 30 boxes.

Place words in the boxes, where the last letter of one becomes the first letter of the next. The words must fit exactly into the 30 boxes.

There are already some letters placed within the boxes. Find words to fit. The given letters can fall anywhere within a word. Use any words you like.

For example:

				T					L				N		

		T				K					

(SHORT, TROUBLE, ESSENCE, EASTER, RANK, KNIGHT)

S	H	O	R	**T**	R	O	U	B	**L**	E	S	S	E	**N**	C	E

A	S	**T**	E	R	A	N	**K**	N	I	G	H	T

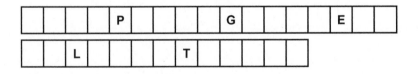

COMBINED ANAGRAMS 8

HOW TO PLAY

Two words have been combined and their letters arranged in alphabetical order.

Can you work out the two words?

For example the words SEVEN and EIGHT would combine to form EEEGHINSTV

Topic: Fruit

	Answer
AELLMPPPU	
AAEEGNOPRR	
AACEEGHPPR	
ACEILMNOOPRT	

QUOTE GRID 8

HOW TO PLAY

Included in the grid is a one sentence quote. The words are in a continuous string, and the first word has been circled.

When you have found the quote, put the small letters from each square in the correct order into the empty grid to find a phrase relating to the quote.

ᴹ DECEMBER	ᴬ WITH	ˢ AN	ᴬ PARTY	[shaded]	ᴺ NEXT	ᴼ THE
ᵀ OF	ᴴ BEGINS	ᶜ (CHRISTMAS)	ᴾ OFFICE	ᴿ AND	ˢ YEAR.	ᴵ FIFTEENTH
ᴿ ABOUT	ˢ FIRST	ᴱ FINALLY	ʸ WHEN	ᵀ ENDS	ᵀ APRIL	ᴿ SPENT,
ᴵ THE	[shaded]	ᶜ YOU	ᴸ REALIZE	ᴱ WHAT	ᴮ YOU	ᴬ AROUND

							[shaded]					
[shaded]	[shaded]											[shaded]

WORD CAPSULE 8

HOW TO PLAY

Choose six 5-letter words that start with the letter on the left and end with the letters on the right. Choose a different word each time.

For example if the capsule was:

H				C
				L
				O
				U
				D
				Y

Your answers may be:

H	A	V	O	C
	O	V	E	L
	E	L	L	O
	A	I	K	U
	A	T	E	D
	U	R	R	Y

B				P
				U
				R
				P
				L
				E

MISSING ALPHABET 8

HOW TO PLAY

All 26 letters of the alphabet have been removed from this passage.

Can you put them in the correct places?

The alphabet is listed so you can cross off each letter as you place it into the passage

T__e __an __elt so de__ected a__d

un__uestiona__ly an__r__ tha__ he so__d h__s

wif__'s pri__ed taxi!

"Perha__s I __an __se the si__teen thou__an__

doll__ __s to ta__e my __ife on __acati__n"

he thought.

ABCDEFGHIJKLMNOPQRSTUVWXYZ

MINI WORD SUDOKU 8

HOW TO PLAY

Place the letters from the 6- letter word **SIGNAL** in the grid so that each column, each row, and each of the six 2×3 sub-grids contains all of the 6 letters from the word.

			L		
	A			G	
	N	A			
L					
S		I			
A					

WORDS FROM A WORD 8

HOW TO PLAY

Choose words that begin with the given letters and fit the category.

For example if the grid contained:

LETTER	CATEGORY	NUMBER OF WORDS
K	Girl's name	1
E	Occupation	2
N	Place name	3
T	Adjective	4

You would need to think of 1 girl's name beginning with K;
2 occupations beginning with; E, 3 place names beginning with N;
4 adjectives beginning with T.

LETTER	CATEGORY	NUMBER OF WORDS	WORDS
N	Scientist	1	
A	Chemical element	2	
P	Emotion	3	
I	Creature	4	
E	Adverb	5	
R	Food	6	

RHYMING WORDS 8

HOW TO PLAY

Find a word that rhymes with the given word and fits the definition.

For example:

WORD	DEFINITION
BARROW	Vegetable

The answer would be
MARROW

WORD	DEFINITION	RHYMING WORD
TAX	Short broad-headed nails	
LEAVE	Arm covering	
TEETH	Open flat tract of land	
BIRTH	Sleeping place on ship	
ROAST	Spirit	
PISTE	Compass point	
FIRST	Most bad	
DRESSED	Invited person	
CASTE	Final	
LEAPT	Cried	

NAMES 8

HOW TO PLAY

Each row has a five-letter boy's name in it with the letters rearranged, plus one extra letter.

Work out the name, then place the extra letter in the right hand column.

Rearrange the extra letters to make another name.

For example:

						Boy's name	Extra letter
E	C	F	A	L	N	LANCE	F

						Boy's name	Extra letter
A	B	L	O	P	T		
A	A	E	T	H	N		
R	C	E	R	B	U		
S	I	L	E	U	W		
A	E	H	H	N	S		
R	I	L	N	C	T		
Additional name							

REMEMBERING NAMES AND FACES 8

There are various strategies for remembering names and faces and we will look at a number of them in these exercises.
They include:

- Repetition
    - Say the name out loud a few times
    - Write the name down a few times
- Association
    - Think about what you are most likely to remember about the person.
    - Associate the name or person with a physical characteristic e.g. rosy cheeks; someone you know; a personal characteristic e.g. smiling Linda; a famous person; a rhyming word e.g. 'Phil' and 'hill'; an item; an occupation.
    - Create a mind picture, the more unusual the better, e.g. imagine a large orange dinosaur wearing a baseball cap with the person's name on the cap

HOW TO PLAY

Choose any strategy for remembering people.

Study the people, remember the names,
then turn over and fill in the sheet.

If you don't remember all the details, do the exercise
again at a later date.

Ida
Driver

Wesley
Fire fighter

Vivienne
Proof reader

Greg
Consultant

Roberta
Surgeon

Pedro
Fish farmer

REMEMBERING NAMES AND FACES 8

These are the six people:

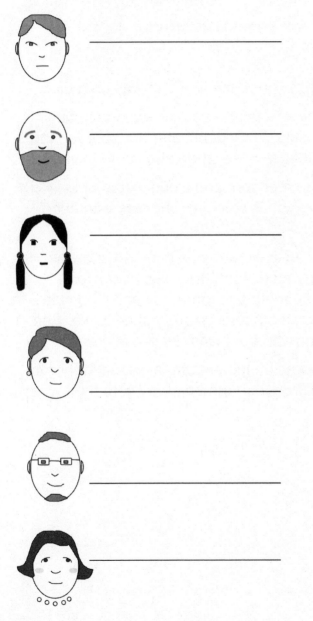

CORRECTING SPELLING 8

HOW TO PLAY

Rewrite the passage, correcting any spelling mistakes.

Julie desided to anounce that she was on a diet.

Her freinds where impresed and woud help out when they could. They didn't ofer her cookys, and only served black cofee when she came to vissit.

Julie liked the atention, and woud instantaniusly start discusing diets wenever she was with her colleages.

Unfortunatly Julie worked in a canteen and was surounded by food. Temtation was everywere: sanwiches, spagetti and tomatoe sauce, pumkin pie, rubarb crumble and rasberry cheescake. She took food from the trolly and ate it in secrete.

Julie's boss was observent and aranged for her to move to a diffrent department, one were their was no food.

WORDSEARCH 8

CONTINUOUS STRING

HOW TO PLAY

The words in the quotation are in a continuous string in the grid (without the punctuation), either horizontally or vertically though not diagonally.

The starting letter is circled.

N	D	E	R	W	N	K	C	I	U
U	A	T	S	A	M	L	O	W	Q
O	N	D	A	L	O	Y	H	A	M
T	S	A	R	E	W	K	G	Z	A
E	N	O	R	V	A	I	N	I	S
L	O	R	E	U	C	D	S	Ⓘ	T
B	W	B	W	U	E	N	L	E	A
A	N	L	O	M	R	A	I	R	R
E	U	E	Y	C	L	E	V	D	N
R	A	T	R	A	C	A	E	O	T

IT'S AMAZING HOW

QUICKLY KIDS LEARN

TO DRIVE A CAR, YET

ARE UNABLE TO

UNDERSTAND A

LAWNMOWER, A

SNOWBLOWER OR

VACUUM CLEANER.

Ben Bergor

WORD LADDER 8

HOW TO PLAY

Turn the first word into the last word by changing a single letter each time, making sure each step is a proper word.

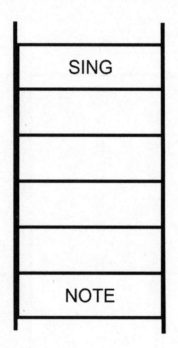

CONTINUOUS WORDS 8

HOW TO PLAY

This is a list of names joined together, with the word spaces removed. How many can you find?

Topic: Household items

armchairradioottomanmicrowavewastebask
ettableornamentlinentowelscandlestick
cookerreclinersetteeshelffutonbureaucouch
hammockhamperrefrigeratorbassinetbook
shelftelevisioncarpethighchairbenchches
tstoollampcomputersofabedclockclosetside
boardmattressbowlbeddeckchaircotfoot
stoolplatescreendishwasherdrapescup
boarddeskjugmirrordivanwritingdesk

WEB WORDS 8

HOW TO PLAY

Fill in each blank square with two letters to form a six letter word with the letters diagonally above and below. The words read downwards.

For example:

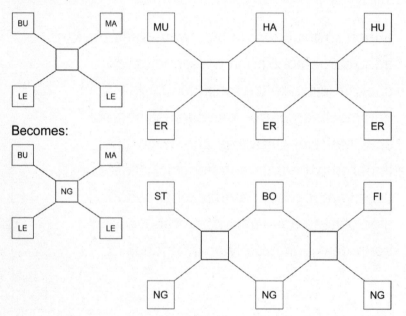

Becomes:

WORD CHAIN 8

HOW TO PLAY

Using one of the words, you have a minute to form a word chain by changing one letter at a time.

Repeat words are not counted.

For example, if the word were RISES, your chain might be:

RIDES, HIDES, HIVES, HIRES, FIRES, FIRMS, FARMS, FORMS, WORMS

If you come to a point where you are unable to make any more words, you can cross off the last word(s) and go back until you can continue the chain, as long as it is within the time limit.

Take a minute for each of the five words.

WAGER	
SEEMS	
CALLS	
BERRY	
WIPER	

SOLVING SENTENCES 8

HOW TO PLAY

What does this sentence say?

I SITE ASYT OREA DTHEF IRSTH ALFON
EWAY, DNUORY AWREH TOE HTFLAH
DNOCESE HTN EH TDNA?

TWISTER 8

HOW TO PLAY

Eight words, each 6 letters long, fit into the grid, in a stepped format.

Four words go downwards and four upwards, with the middle letters being shared.

One letter is given.

If the grid and words were:

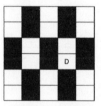

INURES, SEDATE

STADIA. STRUTS

The answer would be:

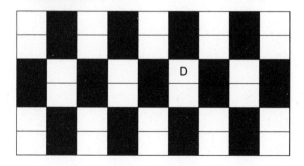

REDDEN

NEEDLE

RAIDER

PATIOS

SODIUM

ELDEST

GUITAR

MUDDLE

TEN ADJECTIVES 8

HOW TO PLAY

Think of 10 adjectives that
start with the letters given.

J	
K	
U	

FIRST LETTER 8

HOW TO PLAY

Change the first letter of each of the words in the group so that all words have the same, new, first letter. Make sure that the new words are proper words, though not proper nouns.

When you have found all the new letters, rearrange them to form a three-letter word.

	NEW LETTER
SINK - WALLET - DULL - HAVE - LOSER	
MEAL - PEST - EITHER - CONE - ROOM	
CRISES - ROTA - CRONY - ODES - FLEX	

Word:

PATTERNS 8

HOW TO PLAY

Can you work out the pattern?

At the top of the first three columns is a name.

In the right hand column are three words that fit into the named categories.

Work out the pattern and place the words into the appropriate boxes in the grid. The first two have been done for you.

KAREN	JENNI	TESSA	category	
			Name of husband	DENNIS CALEB DEAN
		BELLAMY	Surname	BELLAMY ELLIS PARKER
			Favorite place	FRANCE ENGLAND DELHI
TRAVEL			Favorite activity	NETBALL SEWING TRAVEL
			Favorite food	HERRING CAKE PEACH

LETTER SQUARES 8

HOW TO PLAY

Choose words that form a square going clockwise: Take the last letter of the given word, and write in a word of the same length starting with this letter and going downwards. Take the last letter of this word and write in another word starting with this letter and going to the left. Finally, take the last letter of this word and write in a word starting with this letter and ending with the first letter of the first word.

For example, if the first was SIT

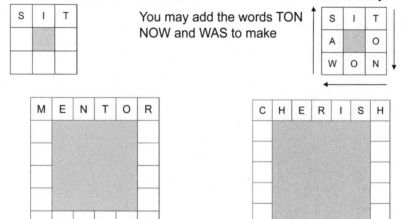

You may add the words TON NOW and WAS to make

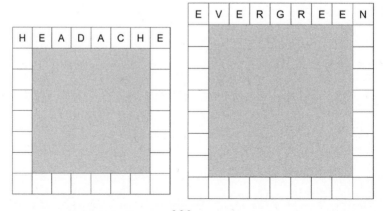

FICTIONAL LANGUAGE 8

HOW TO PLAY

A few words have been translated from English into a fictional language

Learn the translated words, then turn the page and fill in the fictional words in the gaps.

English	Fictional language
CLASS	KLASELEA
DRESSES	MAGDAJUX
FEET	PAAPIEX
MUSIC	HIMIMU

FICTIONAL LANGUAGE 8
Text

She loved going to watch the dance competitions.

The women wore beautiful _____, the men looked very smart, and she liked listening to the lively _____.

She wished she had gone to dance _____ when she was younger, but always felt like she had two left _____.

Level 9

WORD TRAIL 9

HOW TO PLAY

Find 5 words in the grid.

Words go vertically, horizontally or diagonally.

Theme: Kitchen items.

C	U	L	A	R	E
E	R	T	P	T	K
R	F	L	E	C	O
I	R	E	R	E	O
G	Y	A	O	L	T
E	R	T	K	E	T

JOINING WORDS 9

HOW TO PLAY

Find a word that completes the first word and begins the second.

The number in brackets indicates the number of letters that are missing.

COU	__ __	EER	(2)
TAB	__ __	MON	(2)
CLOS	__ __	HER	(2)
DRA	__ __ __	KY	(3)
CAR	__ __ __	ITION	(3)
CH	__ __ __	PORT	(3)
ST	__ __ __ __	TRIP	(4)
PAIN	__ __ __ __	LE	(4)
PIC	__ __ __ __	EN	(4)

PYRAMID WORDS 9

HOW TO PLAY

Fill in the rows with words that start with the letters given.

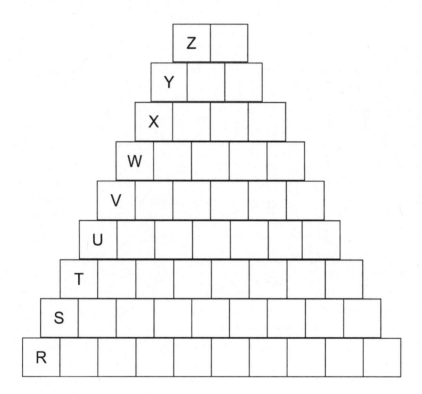

LETTER CROSS 9

HOW TO PLAY

Cross out the letters that appear four times.

The remaining letters spell the name of a musical instrument.

Q	K	W	H	B	Z	M	E	X	N
O		F	Z	S	P	V	F	D	C
D	B	E	C	L	K	U	M	Y	V
H	W	M	Q	A	X	C	N	O	K
S	J	Y	N	Z	F		J	Q	
L	P	T	H	D	V	O	K	S	E
X	C	B	O	S	E	G		P	Y
F	N	W	L	X	J	Y	M	I	Z
J	V	D	P	R	Q	L	W	B	H

SPEED WORDS 9

HOW TO PLAY

Choose 10 words that fit the criteria given.

Choose words that are not proper nouns.

Use a different word for each question.

Choose a word that:		
1	Begins with "PS" and ends in "Y"	
2	Contains 2 "U"s, ends in "S," and is not a plural	
3	Contains 'Y' and 'X' and has 3 syllables	
4	Fits into "__ A __ O __ E"	
5	Starts and ends with "SH" and has two syllables	
6	Is an anagram of "NONOTOP"	
7	Rhymes with "FRESH"	
8	A palindrome that means "relating to a city or town"	
9	Has more than 9 letters and starts with "T"	
10	Has 4 letters, 3 of which are vowels	

WORKING IT OUT 9

HOW TO PLAY

Work out what is these sentences have in common.

The salesmen were nameless.

A teardrop fell on the predator.

The rattles will startle her.

He secured the rescued puppy.

Don't arrest the rarest one.

She teased the sedate lady.

The hardest part was trashed.

X WORDS 9

HOW TO PLAY

Place the correct words in the rows in the grid so that both diagonals spell a five-letter word reading from top to bottom.

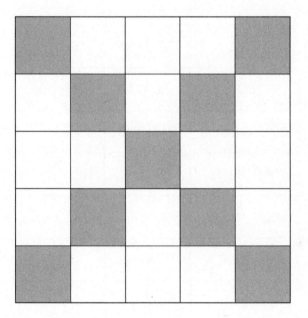

FLASH

PRONG

EPOCH

SPACE

MERRY

SYNONYMS 9

HOW TO PLAY

Find the twelve matching pairs of synonyms in the grid.

Rearrange the four remaining words to form a sentence

DISCIPLINE	SAD	GENUINE	RICH
COMMON	HIGH	LOYAL	SLENDER
BRAIN	COURTEOUS	FAMOUS	WEAK
SLIM	IMPOLITE	USUAL	HELPING
REAL	WELL-KNOWN	SLEEPY	POLITE
TALL	FEEBLE	FAITHFUL	YOUR
DROWSY	RUDE	WEALTHY	UNHAPPY

Sentence: _____ _____

_____ _____

FIRST AND LAST LETTERS 9

HOW TO PLAY

Think of 10 words where the first and last letters alternate.

For example, if the first word is "REALLY," the next word would need to start with Y and end with R, the third word would then start with R and end with Y again, and so on.

Example: REALLY – YOUR – RAY – YONDER – RARITY – YEAR – RATIFY – YOUNGER – ROMANY – YOUNGSTER

Using the given words, find another 9 words with alternating first and last letters.

For words ending in S, aim to avoid using plurals.

LEMON	
NODDING	
TEN	

SPLIT WORDS 9

HOW TO PLAY

There are four 8-letter words that have been split into 2-letter pieces.

Find the matching parts of the four words.

Topic: Occupations

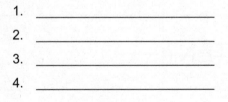

CI	OR	RE	MU
SS	SC	MI	IT
UL	ST	SI	NI
ER	PT	WA	AN

1. _____

2. _____

3. _____

4. _____

MEMORY GRID 9

HOW TO PLAY

Study the grid, and remember the position of the words.

Then turn the page and answer the questions.

Topic: Numbers

		ELEVEN		
		EIGHT		
TWENTY	TWO	SEVEN	ONE	SIX
		FIFTEEN		
		THIRTEEN		
		THIRTY		

MEMORY GRID 9

Questions

1. Which number is directly below SEVEN?

2. Which number is two to the right of the center number?

3. Which number is at the top?

4. Which number is immediately to the left of TWO?

5. Which number is three places above THIRTEEN?

6. Which number is four places below EIGHT?

7. What would you get if you add up the bottom two numbers?

DEFINITIONS 9

HOW TO PLAY

Choose the correct definition for each word.

Rampart
Flourishing or spreading in an uncontrolled way

Rush around in a violent way

A wall built to defend a castle

Pachyderm
A skin disorder

A large animal with thick skin

Special gauze for covering skin lesions

Ligature
A cord used to tie up a bleeding artery

A short band of tissue connecting bones or cartilages

Written works with artistic merit

Duiker
African antelope

A man holding the highest hereditary title in Britain

A musical instrument

Vermiform
Pasta made in long thin threads

Having the form of a worm

Creature that harms crops and carries disease

Yawl
A harsh cry for help

A contagious tropical disease

A sailing boat with two masts

Mycology
Pain in a muscle or group of muscles

Short sightedness

The scientific study of fungi

Gesso
A hard compound of plaster of Paris used in sculpture

A movement of part of the body to express meaning

A knitted garment

Morpheme
A drug obtained from opium

The smallest unit of meaning that a word can be divided into

To change smoothly

Claymore
A large type of sword used in Scotland

An earthenware pot

A small brick building

COLUMN WORDS 9

HOW TO PLAY

Place the words in the correct rows in the grid so that columns 2 and 5 spell out six-letter words.

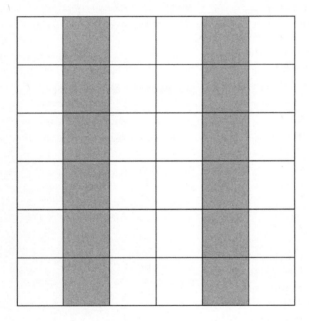

SWOOSH

SELLER

STORMY

INCOME

TISSUE

ERRORS

STRINGS 9

HOW TO PLAY

The grid has 30 boxes.

Place words in the boxes, where the last letter of one becomes the first letter of the next. The words must fit exactly into the 30 boxes.

There are already some letters placed within the boxes. Find words to fit. The given letters can fall anywhere within a word. Use any words you like.

For example:

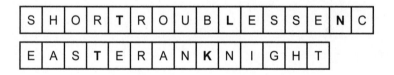

(SHORT, TROUBLE, ESSENCE, EASTER, RANK, KNIGHT)

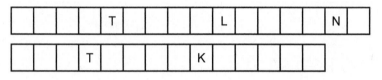

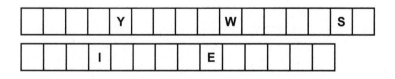

COMBINED ANAGRAMS 9

HOW TO PLAY

Two words have been combined and their letters arranged in alphabetical order.

Can you work out the two words?

For example the words SEVEN and EIGHT would combine to form EEEGHINSTV

Topic: Sea animals

	Answer
AABCELRS	
ADEHILQSUW	
ABEHKLORRSST	
CEOOOPRSSTTUY	

QUOTE GRID 9

HOW TO PLAY

Included in the grid is a one sentence quote. The words are in a continuous string, and the first word has been circled.

When you have found the quote, put the small letters from each square in the correct order into the empty grid to find a phrase relating to the quote.

N TO	E CONTRARY	M TRIVIA!	E WITH	T PEOPLE
T THE		V MORE	Y TORMENTING	S THE
T THE	O ORGANIZATION	D IS	A NOTHING	S JUST
F OF	H MIND,	E MEMORY,		C IT'S
E OF	M THE	T OF	R THE	I IMAGINATION...

WORD CAPSULE 9

HOW TO PLAY

Choose six 5-letter words that start with the letter on the left and end with the letters on the right. Choose a different word each time.

For example if the capsule was:

H				C
				L
				O
				U
				D
				Y

Your answers may be:

H	A	V	O	C
	O	V	E	L
	E	L	L	O
	A	I	K	U
	A	T	E	D
	U	R	R	Y

K				H
				A
				N
				D
				L
				E

W				Z
				E
				P
				H
				Y
				R

MISSING ALPHABET 9

HOW TO PLAY

All 26 letters of the alphabet have been removed from this passage.

Can you put them in the correct places?

The alphabet is listed so you can cross off each letter as you place it into the passage

His wife was livid!

She jumped and screamed like a crazy woman!

"You get my taxi back instantly!" she squealed, hurling an ax at him ferociously.

ABCDEFGHIJKLMNOPQRSTUVWXYZ

MINI WORD SUDOKU 9

HOW TO PLAY

Place the letters from the 6- letter word **JARGON** in the grid so that each column, each row, and each of the six 2×3 sub-grids contains all of the 6 letters from the word.

		A		N	
		R	A		
					O
			R	A	
	G		O		
J					

WORDS FROM A WORD 9

HOW TO PLAY

Choose words that begin with the given letters and fit the category.

For example if the grid contained:

LETTER	CATEGORY	NUMBER OF WORDS
K	Girl's name	1
E	Occupation	2
N	Place name	3
T	Adjective	4

You would need to think of 1 girl's name beginning with K;
2 occupations beginning with; E, 3 place names beginning with N;
4 adjectives beginning with T.

LETTER	CATEGORY	NUMBER OF WORDS	WORDS
Q	Bird	1	
U	Language	2	
E	Part of the body	3	
B	Occupation	4	
E	Six letter word	5	
C	Chemical element	6	

RHYMING WORDS 9

HOW TO PLAY

Find a word that rhymes with the given word and fits the definition.

For example:

WORD	DEFINITION
BARROW	Vegetable

The answer would be
MARROW

WORD	DEFINITION	RHYMING WORD
BREAST	Compass point	
FRONT	Not sharp	
MEANT	Coin	
FAINT	Sham attack, pretence	
MOULT	Young horse	
BUILT	Cast off lover	
DEALT	Become liquefied	
CHECKED	Faction	
FLUTE	Footwear	
DROUGHT	Person seeking information	

NAMES 9

HOW TO PLAY

Each row has a five-letter girl's name in it with the letters rearranged, plus one extra letter.

Work out the name, then place the extra letter in the right hand column.

Rearrange the extra letters to make another name.

For example:

						Girl's name	Extra letter
M	A	M	E	S	G	GEMMA	S

						Girl's name	Extra letter
P	I	L	E	A	C		
Y	T	E	L	B	T		
O	I	R	I	S	D		
C	K	A	N	J	Y		
E	E	U	N	L	L		
C	E	V	Y	I	K		
R	Y	D	A	U	T		
Additional name							

REMEMBERING NAMES AND FACES 9

There are various strategies for remembering names and faces and we will look at a number of them in these exercises.
They include:

- Repetition
    - Say the name out loud a few times
    - Write the name down a few times
- Association
    - Think about what you are most likely to remember about the person.
    - Associate the name or person with a physical characteristic e.g. rosy cheeks; someone you know; a personal characteristic e.g. smiling Linda; a famous person; a rhyming word e.g. 'Phil' and 'hill'; an item; an occupation.
    - Create a mind picture, the more unusual the better, e.g. imagine a large orange dinosaur wearing a baseball cap with the person's name on the cap

HOW TO PLAY

Choose any strategy for remembering people.

Brett
Fundraiser
From Maine

Georgia
Artist
From Utah

Angel
Chef
From Vermont

Ethel
Retired teacher
From Montana

Constance
Surveyor
From Illinois

Raul
Mechanic
From Maine

Jackie
Nurse
From Montana

Ryan
Cake maker
From Indiana

REMEMBERING NAMES AND FACES 9

These are the eight people:

351

CORRECTING SPELLING 9

HOW TO PLAY

Rewrite the passage, correcting any spelling mistakes.

Carlos looked at the calender and started to panick. Tomorow was the twelth, his wedding aniversery, and he had forgoten!

He would definately be in truoble if he meerley gave his wife a card. A big arguement would be a certanty.

Carlos found he could excell at times like this. He could usally devize a sucessful solution.

Quickly he called a restarant, one with a foriegn name, wich he beleived sounded more romantic. He booked a pink metalic limosine and orderd lilac fushias.

Thier evening was a genuin succes.

"Thanks for a terific time" said his wife "your grate at planning suprises in advanse."

WORDSEARCH 9

SQUARE WORDS

HOW TO PLAY

All words are girls' names, are 8 letters long and are placed in the grid in the shape of a square.

For example, the name FLORENCE would be found:

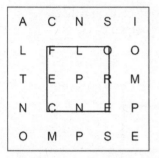

Letters go clockwise or anticlockwise, and the first letter can be found at any point in the square.

BEATRICE

CAROLINE

DOROTHEA

FELICITY

JENNIFER

MARGARET

PATRICIA

WORD LADDER 9
CODE WORD

HOW TO PLAY

This is a word ladder puzzle with a difference.

Each of the words is in code.

To solve the puzzle, work out the code, then change a single letter each time, making sure each step is a proper word.

TIPQ
SBJE

CONTINUOUS WORDS 9

HOW TO PLAY

This is a list of names joined together, with the word spaces removed. How many can you find?

Topic: Words containing the letter X

coccyxannexflexexcelexceptanorexiaconvex
vixenintoxicateddetoxoxideelixirrelaxapexgal
axysixteennexttuxedoonyxluxuryinfluxindexe
xempttextwaxyvortexexamsfixatetoxiccalixex
citingcrucifixexitoxtaillexiconoxygenexistingfo
xgloverouxproxysyntaxhexagonthoraxhoaxx
enophobiaapproximateextenddextroussphinx
matrixprefixtaxipixiesperoxideexportparadox
boxingcoaxedmixturemaxim

WEB WORDS 9

HOW TO PLAY

Fill in each blank square with two letters to form a six letter word with the letters diagonally above and below. The words read downwards.

For example:

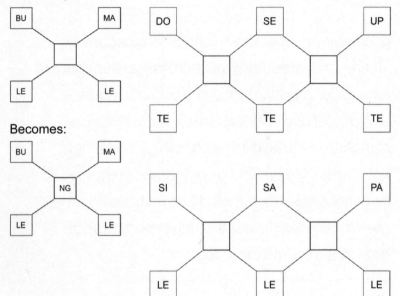

Becomes:

WORD CHAIN 9

HOW TO PLAY

Using one of the words, you have a minute to form a word chain by changing one letter at a time.

Repeat words are not counted.

For example, if the word were RISES, your chain might be:

RIDES, HIDES, HIVES, HIRES, FIRES, FIRMS, FARMS, FORMS, WORMS

If you come to a point where you are unable to make any more words, you can cross off the last word(s) and go back until you can continue the chain, as long as it is within the time limit.

Take a minute for each of the five words.

THINK	
COULD	
PLEAS	
NEVER	
SCARE	

SOLVING SENTENCES 9

HOW TO PLAY

What does this sentence say?

MITE MITE VAST NOD TUB LYRE BRACE NO POT SEW

TWISTER 9

HOW TO PLAY

Eight words, each 6 letters long, fit into the grid, in a stepped format.

Four words go downwards and four upwards, with the middle letters being shared.

One letter is given.

If the grid and words were:

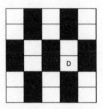

INURES, SEDATE
STADIA. STRUTS

The answer would be:

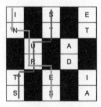

AMORAL

CINEMA

LATEST

ATOMIC

STRONG

REMOVE

GNETUM

EVENTS

TEN ADJECTIVES 9

HOW TO PLAY

Think of 10 adjectives that start with the letters given.

Q	
Y	

FIRST LETTER 9

HOW TO PLAY

Change the first letter of each of the words in the group so that all words have the same, new, first letter. Make sure that the new words are proper words, though not proper nouns.

When you have found all the new letters, rearrange them to form a four-letter word.

	NEW LETTER
FOOT - PILE - DEAR - GULL - HARK	
FOOD - HEAR - MALE - SILL - LUST	
NOOK - BAKE - TINE - PEEK - SUMP	
SON - CRATE - ETCH - STEM - ORE	

Word:

PATTERNS 9

HOW TO PLAY

Can you work out the pattern?

At the top of the first three columns is a name.

In the right hand column are three words that fit into the named categories.

Work out the pattern and place the words into the appropriate boxes in the grid. The first two have been done for you.

ANNA	DIANE	KIM	category	
			Name of husband	HENRI BOB LEON
			Favorite place	LINCOLN MILTON NORTHAMPTON
GARDENING			Favorite activity	GARDENING ENGINEERING FARMING
			Favorite creature	DOVE JACKAL REINDEER
	HINDI		Favorite language	FRENCH URDU HINDI

LETTER SQUARES 9

HOW TO PLAY

Choose words that form a square going clockwise: Take the last letter of the given word, and write in a word of the same length starting with this letter and going downwards. Take the last letter of this word and write in another word starting with this letter and going to the left. Finally, take the last letter of this word and write in a word starting with this letter and ending with the first letter of the first word.

For example, if the first was SIT

You may add the words TON NOW and WAS to make

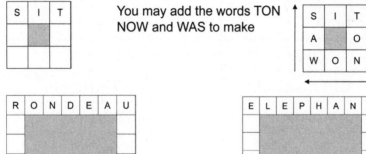

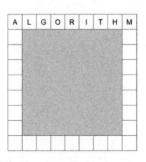

FICTIONAL LANGUAGE 9

HOW TO PLAY

A few words have been translated from English into a fictional language

Learn the translated words, then turn the page and fill in the fictional words in the gaps.

English	Fictional language
AFRICA	APRUGA
BOAT	BANGKABAT
CROCODILES	BUWAYAX
HOT	MAINCHAU
PHOTOS	LITRATOX

FICTIONAL LANGUAGE 9
Text

It was his first trip to _____

and he was enjoying the

_____ weather. The

river looked beautiful and he decided to go

on a _____ trip.

It wasn't safe to swim in the river as there

were _____

basking at the water's edge, but he

got out his camera and took plenty of

_____.

Level 10

WORD TRAIL 10

HOW TO PLAY

Find 6 words in the grid.

Words go vertically, horizontally or diagonally.

Theme: Shapes

L	A	E	C	R	I
R	S	L	N	A	C
I	Q	G	I	R	T
P	S	U	L	L	A
O	L	A	R	E	V
N	G	B	O	E	O

JOINING WORDS 10

HOW TO PLAY

Find a word that completes the first word and begins the second.

The number in brackets indicates the number of letters that are missing.

RAN	__ __	EESE	(2)
SCA	__ __	RIC	(2)
MON	__ __	ELASH	(2)
TUR	__ __ __	RING	(3)
US	__ __ __	MIT	(3)
ZEA	__ __ __	US	(3)
PE	__ __ __ __	LIS	(4)
TH	__ __ __ __	HOG	(4)
W	__ __ __ __	ON	(4)

PYRAMID WORDS 10

HOW TO PLAY

Fill in the rows with words that start with the letters given.

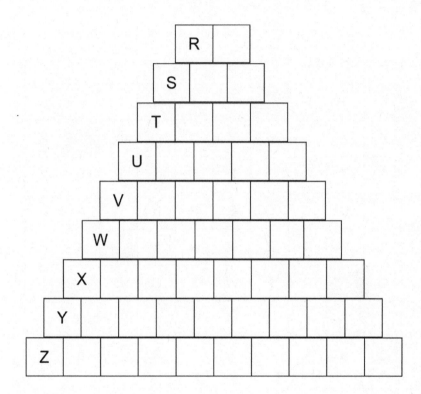

LETTER CROSS 10

HOW TO PLAY

Cross out the letters that appear four times.

The remaining letters spell the name of a river.

R	D	V	Q	B	L	W	H	J	V
N	J	P		C	Y	U	F	G	N
F	Z	L	J	X	S	Q	O		K
G	T	W	U	F	I	X	R	B	Y
I	Q	C	O	B	P	K	W	A	L
K	Y	D	Z	V	N	Y		X	P
O		R	F	W	Z	G	O	D	I
E	G	L	Z	M	I	J	U	Q	V
C	U	K	C	X	D	R	P	B	N

SPEED WORDS 10

HOW TO PLAY

Choose 10 words that fit the criteria given.

Choose words that are not proper nouns.

Use a different word for each question.

Choose a word that:		
1	Has 4 syllables and ends in "O"	
2	Has 4 letters in reverse alphabetical order	
3	Starts and ends with the letters "ING"	
4	Is an anagram of "ZIEMAAKK"	
5	Is the name of a fruit and is also an anagram of a word meaning "unit of linear measurement"	
6	Has 5 syllables and starts with "U"	
7	Rhymes with "CHERISH"	
8	Is a homophone of "MARSHAL"	
9	Fits into "S __ S __ __ __ __ C"	
10	Contains this combination of letters together "THH"	

WORKING IT OUT 10

HOW TO PLAY

Work out what is unusual about this passage.

Tim says "Hello" but Mike snubs him.

Joan likes Tim. Mike feels he's very blunt.

"You can't upset him" Joan sighs, "he's kind, happy but very gruff."

X WORDS 10

HOW TO PLAY

Place the correct words in the rows in the grid so that both diagonals spell a five-letter word reading from top to bottom.

SWILL

BELOW

ELATE

MESHY

STAGE

SYNONYMS 10

HOW TO PLAY

Find the twelve matching pairs of synonyms in the grid.

Rearrange the four remaining words to form a sentence

EMPOWERED	NAIVE	EXCESSIVE	COMPLETE
CHALLENGES	UNMISTAKABLE	IMMINENT	MALEVOLENT
CUSTOMARY	MERCIFUL	FAVORABLE	EXTENSIVE
TEMPTING	MALICIOUS	HABITUAL	OBVIOUS
IMPENDING	AUTHORIZED	GULLIBLE	FLORID
EXORBITANT	THE	CLEMENT	FUN
FLUSHED	WIDESPREAD	OPPORTUNE	ENTICING

Sentence: _____ _____

_____ _____

FIRST AND LAST LETTERS 10

HOW TO PLAY

Think of 10 words where the first and last letters alternate.

For example, if the first word is "REALLY," the next word would need to start with Y and end with R, the third word would then start with R and end with Y again, and so on.

Example: REALLY – YOUR –
RAY – YONDER – RARITY – YEAR – RATIFY – YOUNGER –
ROMANY – YOUNGSTER

Using the given words, find another 9 words with alternating first and last letters.

For words ending in S, aim to avoid using plurals.

EGRESS	
ARM	
COAL	

SPLIT WORDS 10

HOW TO PLAY

There are four 8-letter words that have been split into 2-letter pieces.

Find the matching parts of the four words.

Topic: Animals

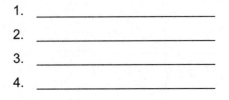

RR	TE	KA	DG
EH	AN	SQ	EL
UI	OO	HE	LO
AR	PE	NG	OG

1. _____
2. _____
3. _____
4. _____

MEMORY GRID 10

HOW TO PLAY

Study the grid, and remember the position of the words.

Then turn the page and answer the questions.

Topic: Positions

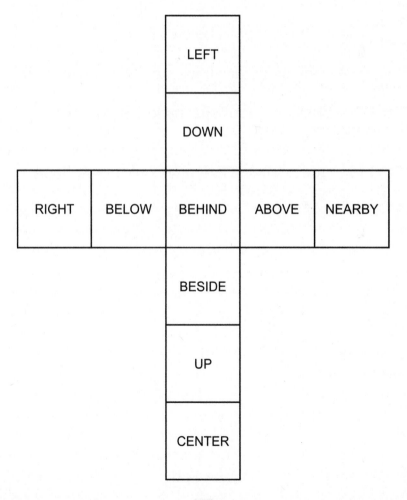

MEMORY GRID 10

Questions

1. Where is CENTER?

2. What is to the left of BELOW?

3. Name the positions that start with a vowel

4. What is three spaces below LEFT?

5. How many of the positions start with the letter B?

6. What position is four spaces to the right of RIGHT?

7. Name the positions that have only one syllable

DEFINITIONS 10

HOW TO PLAY

Choose the correct definition for each word.

Fletcher
Ornament in shape of flower
Butcher
Maker of arrows

Jussive
Exercise of authority in maintenance of right
Expressing a command
Being versed in law

Demagogue
Leader of the populace
Partly divine being
Person who studies birth and death statistics

Kibble
To grind coarsely
Communal farming settlement in Israel
To bite cautiously

Primogenitor
Offspring of a person
Existing from the beginning
Earliest ancestor

Sirdar
Large, long-necked Indian lute
Person in command
Short track by railway line

Whelm
Marine gastropod
Engulf, submerge
Young dog, pup

Presage
Exertion of continuous force
Omen, portent
An introduction

Festal
Of a feast
To become poisonous
Rejoicing, joyous

Apodal
Point furthest from earth
Clearly established
Without feet

COLUMN WORDS 10

HOW TO PLAY

Place the words in the correct rows in the grid so that columns 2 and 5 spell out sixletter words.

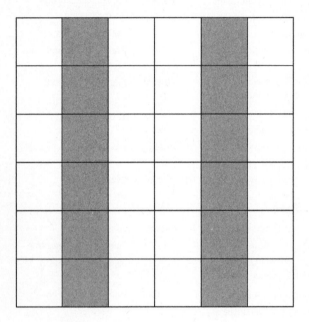

STUPOR

PANICS

SHANDY

CHEERS

ALLOTS

YELLOW

STRINGS 10

HOW TO PLAY

The grid has 30 boxes.

Place words in the boxes, where the last letter of one becomes the first letter of the next. The words must fit exactly into the 30 boxes.

There are already some letters placed within the boxes. Find words to fit. The given letters can fall anywhere within a word. Use any words you like.

For example:

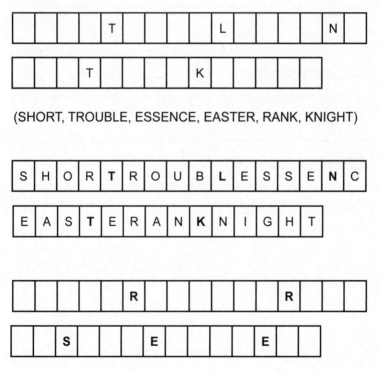

(SHORT, TROUBLE, ESSENCE, EASTER, RANK, KNIGHT)

S	H	O	R	T	R	O	U	B	L	E	S	S	E	N	C

E	A	S	T	E	R	A	N	K	N	I	G	H	T

COMBINED ANAGRAMS 10

HOW TO PLAY

Two words have been combined and their letters arranged in alphabetical order.

Can you work out the two words?

For example the words SEVEN and EIGHT would combine to form EEEGHINSTV

Topic: Modes of transport

	Answer
ACGKNORTUW	
AAAEIILNNPRRT	
CEEEHIILLNOPRRT	
ABBCCEEIILMNRSUY	

QUOTE GRID 10

HOW TO PLAY

Included in the grid is a one sentence quote. The words are in a continuous string, and the first word has been circled.

When you have found the quote, put the small letters from each square in the correct order into the empty grid to find a phrase relating to the quote.

M ARE	E YOU	T ELSE,	F YOURSELF	G THAN	A OBTRUSIVE
O REALLY	T IF	F MAKE	E ANYBODY	R MORE	T (YOU)
M GET	V GOING	U TO		H HAVE	B MAKE
E TO	E YOUR	S HAVE	S ELSE,	R MORE	E TO
T REALIZED.	N REFORM	H YOU	I ANYBODY	T THAN	I NOISE

WORD CAPSULE 10

HOW TO PLAY

Choose six 5-letter words that start with the letter on the left and end with the letters on the right. Choose a different word each time.

For example if the capsule was:

Your answers may be:

H				C
				L
				O
				U
				D
				Y

H	A	V	O	C
	O	V	E	L
	E	L	L	O
	A	I	K	U
	A	T	E	D
	U	R	R	Y

R				P
				E
				N
				C
				I
				L

I				E
				X
				C
				E
				L
				S

MISSING ALPHABET 10

HOW TO PLAY

All 26 letters of the alphabet have been removed from this passage.

Can you put them in the correct places?

The alphabet is listed so you can cross off each letter as you place it into the passage

The man was ama__ ed at he__ e__ trem__ rea__ tion.

"__ arlin__ , I'__ sorr__ " __ e s__ id __ __ ietly.

"As __ t's so im__ ortant to you, I'd li__ e to of__ er to

__ uy a __ axi bet__ een us a__ d __ oin the __ ocal

Taxi Lo__ ers' As__ ociati__ n.

ABCDEFGHIJKLMNOPQRSTUVWXYZ

MINI WORD SUDOKU 10

HOW TO PLAY

Place the letters from the 6- letter word **BRAINS** in the grid so that each column, each row, and each of the six 2×3 sub-grids contains all of the 6 letters from the word.

I					
R	B				
			B	A	
					S
	R		N		
	I			S	

WORDS FROM A WORD 10

HOW TO PLAY

Choose words that begin with the given letters and fit the category.

For example if the grid contained:

LETTER	CATEGORY	NUMBER OF WORDS
K	Girl's name	1
E	Occupation	2
N	Place name	3
T	Adjective	4

You would need to think of 1 girl's name beginning with K;
2 occupations beginning with; E, 3 place names beginning with N;
4 adjectives beginning with T.

LETTER	CATEGORY	NUMBER OF WORDS	WORDS
M	Roman god	1	
O	Mammal	2	
B	Composer	3	
I	Eight letter word	4	
L	Country	5	
E	Food	6	

RHYMING WORDS 10

HOW TO PLAY

Find a word that rhymes with the given word and fits the definition.

For example:

WORD	DEFINITION
BARROW	Vegetable

The answer would be
MARROW

WORD	DEFINITION	RHYMING WORD
SUIT	Attractive	
FLOUT	Uncertainty	
VOTE	Castle ditch	
HEIGHT	Wind toy	
SUITE	Road	
DEBT	Skin moisture	
WEIGHT	Defer action	
POSH	Crush	
GREASE	Relative	
GRAPE	Gauze-like fabric	

NAMES 10

HOW TO PLAY

Each row has a five-letter girl's name in it with the letters rearranged, plus one extra letter.

Work out the name, then place the extra letter in the right hand column.

Rearrange the extra letters to make another name.

For example:

						Girl's name	Extra letter
M	A	M	E	S	G	GEMMA	S

						Girl's name	Extra letter
U	L	P	A	A	Z		
L	H	E	T	S	E		
S	N	A	O	N	Y		
Y	L	E	O	L	H		
U	S	P	T	Y	A		
E	Y	N	I	M	L		
E	A	S	O	R	I		
Additional name							

REMEMBERING NAMES AND FACES 10

There are various strategies for remembering names and faces and we will look at a number of them in these exercises.
They include:
- Repetition
  - Say the name out loud a few times
  - Write the name down a few times
- Association
  - Think about what you are most likely to remember about the person.
  - Associate the name or person with a physical characteristic e.g. rosy cheeks; someone you know; a personal characteristic e.g. smiling Linda; a famous person; a rhyming word e.g. 'Phil' and 'hill'; an item; an occupation.
  - Create a mind picture, the more unusual the better, e.g. imagine a large orange dinosaur wearing a baseball cap with the person's name on the cap

HOW TO PLAY

Choose any strategy for remembering people.

Study the people, remember the names, then turn over and fill in the sheet.

If you don't remember all the details, do the exercise again at a later date.

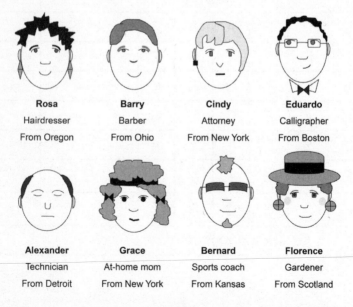

Rosa	**Barry**	**Cindy**	**Eduardo**
Hairdresser	Barber	Attorney	Calligrapher
From Oregon	From Ohio	From New York	From Boston

Alexander	**Grace**	**Bernard**	**Florence**
Technician	At-home mom	Sports coach	Gardener
From Detroit	From New York	From Kansas	From Scotland

390

REMEMBERING NAMES AND FACES 10

These are the eight people:

CORRECTING SPELLING 10

HOW TO PLAY

Rewrite the passage, correcting any spelling mistakes.

Nothing seemd to embaress Lizzy. She was fun, mischevious and laughed a lot. Atempts to dicipline her at school failed, but teachers liked her nontheless.

Wenever she had some musical equipement she would brake into song and turn every sittuation into a karoake.

While Lizzy was at the libary her freinds placed an enormus zylophone on her desk and waited with baited breathe to see her reaction.

Lizzy retourned to her desk. Unpeturbed, and with her usuel abundance of enthuseiasm, she picked up the malets and showed herself to be a connoisuer of the instruement.

The concensus of opinion was that Lizzy was an exeptionally gifted musicien.

WORDSEARCH 10
TWO GRIDS

HOW TO PLAY

Half of the words are in one grid and half in the other.

Words are placed in the grids vertically, horizontally or diagonally.

Y	R	U	L	E	R
P	K	S	E	D	Y
N	R	C	M	O	R
O	M	E	M	E	E
G	N	I	P	Y	T
E	C	Y	H	A	U
P	T	N	I	R	P
A	S	F	C	O	M
T	H	R	E	M	O
L	T	R	A	H	C

P	O	T	P	A	L
E	D	S	P	L	M
N	E	J	T	A	J
C	O	U	R	W	O
I	T	K	D	R	T
L	E	R	F	I	T
R	K	I	S	T	E
E	R	A	S	E	R
C	P	H	O	N	E
L	L	C	J	F	T

CHAIR	LAPTOP	RULER
CHART	MARKER	TAPE
COMPUTER	PAPER	TYPE
DESK	PENCIL	
ERASER	PHONE	TYPING
JOTTER	PRINT	WRITE

WORD LADDER 10
CODE WORD

HOW TO PLAY

This is a word ladder puzzle with a difference.

Each of the words is in code.

To solve the puzzle, work out the code, then change a single letter each time, making sure each step is a proper word.

IFBE

GPPU

CONTINUOUS WORDS 10

HOW TO PLAY

This is a list of names joined together, with the word spaces removed. How many can you find?

Topic: Words containing the letter Z

amazeeczemaamazinggazebooozessyzygy
wizardryfizzyfrenzyfloozyjazzyrazzmatazztop
azzanybuzzerrazorzigguratwaltzzeroozonee
nzymefriezefrozenzephyrmaizemuzzlehazeg
litzyzabaglionecrazelizarddazeddozenzinnia
pizzaplazazirconiafrizzzestyzigzaggizmohert
zzoologyzebralazulisqueezesnoozedgeezer
zillionzeppelinchintzzealousschmaltzzucchin
iseizezenithsneezedbronzezodiaczinggazum
pshowbizzombievizierkazoozoomszonedsiz
eblitzblazegazeszippy

WEB WORDS 10

HOW TO PLAY

Fill in each blank square with two letters to form a six letter word with the letters diagonally above and below. The words read downwards.

For example:

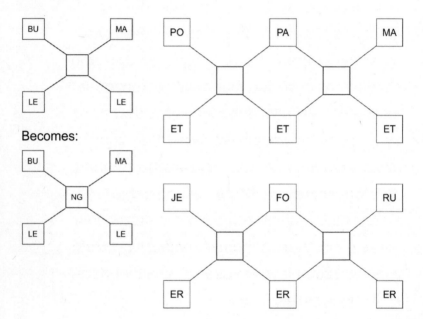

Becomes:

WORD CHAIN 10

HOW TO PLAY

Using one of the words, you have a minute to form a word chain by changing one letter at a time.

Repeat words are not counted.

For example, if the word were SHAPES, your chain might be:

SHARES, SHAKES,
SNAKES, SNARES,
SPARES, SPADES

If you come to a point where you are unable to make any more words, you can cross off the last word(s) and go back until you can continue the chain, as long as it is within the time limit.

Take a minute for each of the five words.

EATING	
TASTES	
FLYING	
PATTED	
STRAWS	

SOLVING SENTENCES 10

HOW TO PLAY

What does this sentence say?

EMO SWORD SERAT HETH GIRWA YDNU
ORWHI LEE MOSAR ETON ANDEC AFT
HERE HTOW AY

TWISTER 10

HOW TO PLAY

Eight words, each 6 letters long, fit into the grid, in a stepped format.

Four words go downwards and four upwards, with the middle letters being shared.

One letter is given.

If the grid and words were:

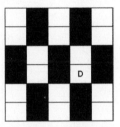

INURES, SEDATE
STADIA. STRUTS

The answer would be:

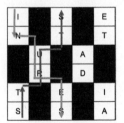

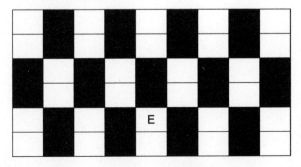

NORMAL

REWORD

REGAIN

DRAWER

FLOWER

NIMROD

REWARD

DRAGON

TEN ADJECTIVES 10

HOW TO PLAY

Think of 10 adjectives that start with the letters given.

X	
Z	

FIRST LETTER 10

HOW TO PLAY

Change the first letter of each of the words in the group so that all words have the same, new, first letter. Make sure that the new words are proper words, though not proper nouns.

When you have found all the new letters, rearrange them to form a four-letter word.

	NEW LETTER
AITCH - COOL - MINE - TRAY - FEAR	
EAST - LORE - CRY - WICK - TEAL	
CRATE - DUNCE - FURS - LAST - BUT	
SEAL - MOVE - OUST - DEED - EAVES	

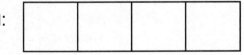

Word:

PATTERNS 10

HOW TO PLAY

Can you work out the pattern?

At the top of the first three columns is a name.

In the right hand column are three words that fit into the named categories.

Work out the pattern and place the words into the appropriate boxes in the grid. The first two have been done for you.

LIZ	COCO	RUTH	category	
			Name of husband	RUSS JOHN MATT
			Surname	POOLE HILL ROSCO
	SOUP		Favorite food	BRAN SOUP MEAT
			Favorite animal	MINK GORILLA DOG
WAIL			Favorite noise	GROAN WAIL PURR

LETTER SQUARES 10

HOW TO PLAY

Choose words that form a square going clockwise: Take the last letter of the given word, and write in a word of the same length starting with this letter and going downwards. Take the last letter of this word and write in another word starting with this letter and going to the left. Finally, take the last letter of this word and write in a word starting with this letter and ending with the first letter of the first word.

For example, if the first was SIT

You may add the words TON NOW and WAS to make

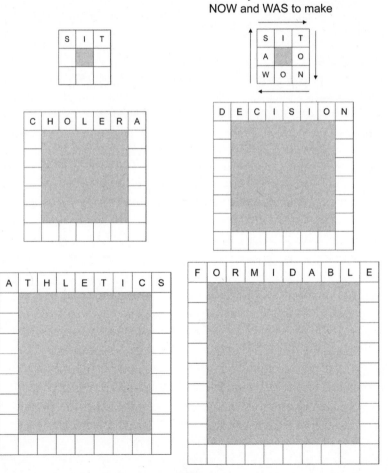

FICTIONAL LANGUAGE 10

HOW TO PLAY

A few words have been translated from English into a fictional language

Learn the translated words, then turn the page and fill in the fictional words in the gaps.

English	Fictional language
FILM	PELIKCIN
LUGGAGE	BAGAQUI
TRAY TABLES	HALAHAX
SEAT BELTS	KULINUPUX
PLANE	EROPLAVI

FICTIONAL LANGUAGE 10
Text

They arrived at the airport and checked in their _____.

Once aboard the _____ they were asked to fasten their

_____.

Part way through watching the

_____,

the food was served on their

_____.

Bonus puzzles

TRIANGLES 1

HOW TO PLAY

Each triangle contains a 3 letter, 4 letter and 5 letter word, placed in the direction of the arrows.

Put the words into the correct triangles.

Example: The words
MAP
CLAP
MUSIC
would be placed:

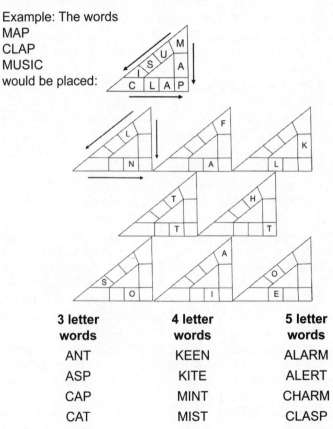

3 letter words	4 letter words	5 letter words
ANT	KEEN	ALARM
ASP	KITE	ALERT
CAP	MINT	CHARM
CAT	MIST	CLASP
FAN	PLOY	FIRST
FLY	PROP	FLOCK
SEE	TRAY	SHARP
SKY	TRIP	STOCK

LETTER SHUFFLE 3

HOW TO PLAY

A saying has been placed in the grid in a continuous string, following the direction of the arrows.

The 7 letters in the shaded squares have been rearranged.

Can you place them in the correct squares and find the saying?

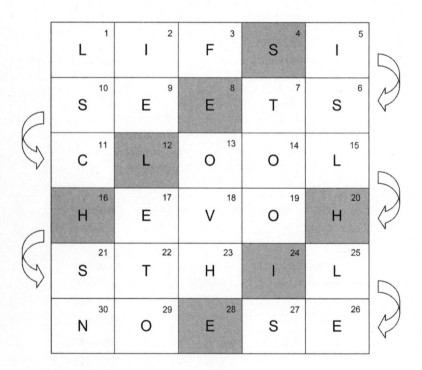

Saying: _____

_____

NINE WORDS 1

HOW TO PLAY

Write a complete sentence with words containing 1 through to 9 letters.

No. of letters	Sentence
1	
2	
3	
4	
5	
6	
7	
8	
9	

Answers

WORD TRAIL 1

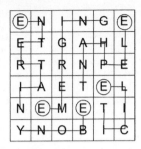

X WORDS 1

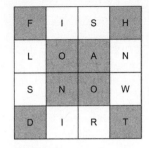

DEFINITIONS 1

Gerbil: Mouse-like rodent; **Jorum:** Large drinking bowl; **Cos:** Kind of lettuce; **Acanthus:** Herbaceous plant: **Pontiff:** The pope; **Milliner:** A person who makes hats; **Beryl:** Transparent mineral; **Yurt:** Tent made of skins or felt: **Flummery:** A soft jelly or porridge made with flour: **Syzygy:** An almost straight-line configuration of three celestial bodies

COLUMN WORDS 1

P	A	R	I	S	H
P	R	E	T	T	Y
P	R	I	O	R	Y
P	E	R	S	O	N
A	S	C	E	N	T
S	T	I	N	G	S

JOINING WORDS 1

DOCT-OR- ANGE; HEAL-TH-IN; NUR-SE-AT; PATI-ENT-AIL; MEDI-CAL-MLY; ILLN-ESS-ENCE; HOSP-ITAL-ICS; MEDI-CINE-MA; THERA-PIST-ON

PYRAMID WORDS 1

There are many acceptable answers. Example:
A, SO, CAR, FLAT, GLORY, YELLOW, RAILWAY, CARRIAGE, GARDENING, ENGAGEMENT

LETTER CROSS 1

NORWAY

SPEED WORDS 1

There are many acceptable answers. Example:
Flower; Meet; Station; Willing; Syntax; Spacious; Razor; Cream; Late; Else

WORKING IT OUT 1

There are no letter "E" s in it

SYNONYMS 1

BIG-LARGE; SMALL-TINY; MESSY-UNTIDY; MAD-ANGRY; LOVING-CARING; CRYING-WEEPING; SLEEPING-SLUMBERING; FAST-QUICK; HORRIBLE-AWFUL; WET-SOGGY
SENTENCE: KEEP TRAINING YOUR BRAIN

FIRST AND LAST LETTERS 1

There are many acceptable answers. Example:
SHOT, TRESS, SPIT, TOSS, SHUT, THIS, SEAT, THUS, SIT, TRUSS
ENTER, RAVE, EAGER, RISE, EVER, RIDE, ENGINEER, ROVE, EASIER, RUSE
POOL, LOOP, PILL, LIMP, PULL, LAMP, PALL, LEAP, PAIL, LISP

SPLIT WORDS 1

BOOT; SHOE; COAT; SOCK; VEST; CAPE; GOWN; BELT

MEMORY GRID 1

1. PINK; 2. YELLOW; 3. BROWN; 4. PURPLE; 5. RED

COMBINED ANAGRAMS 1

TEN TWELVE; ELEVEN SIX; FIFTY FOUR

QUOTE GRID 1

QUOTE: THAT'S ONE SMALL STEP FOR MAN, A GIANT LEAP FOR MANKIND, Neil Armstrong
PHRASE: MOON LANDING

WORD CAPSULE 1

There are many acceptable answers. Example:
HILLS; HEART; HOVER; HEDGE; HENCE; HABIT

MISSING ALPHABET 1

Manuel lived in an apartment on the sixth floor so he was surprised to hear the sound of a very large animal coming from the adjoining apartment. Amazed, he couldn't think of a logical reason for this, so quickly went next door to find out. What animal could it be?

411

MINI WORD SUDOKU 1

E	I	C	P	L	N
N	P	L	C	I	E
C	L	I	E	N	P
P	N	E	I	C	L
L	C	P	N	E	I
I	E	N	L	P	C

WORDS FROM A WORD 1

There are many acceptable answers. Example:
Kangaroo
Austria, Australia
Nectarine, nachos, noodles
Sam, Steven, Simon, Sean
Alice, Anne, Angela, Andrea, Abigail
Singer, sign writer, swim instructor, secretary, surgeon, surveyor

RHYMING WORDS 1

TABLE, HATE, LEEK, HOUR, MIGHT, FUN, HIGHER, BONE, YEW, MISSED

NAMES 1

Girl's name	Extra letter
SALLY	N
DONNA	L
HELEN	C
LINDA	I
SUSAN	O
TANIA	E
NICOLE	

REMEMBERING NAMES AND FACES 1

Rosie; Gordon; Eve; Cameron.

CORRECTING SPELLING 1

<u>Yesterday</u> I went <u>to</u> the mall. One of the <u>chain</u> stores had a twenty <u>per</u> cent off <u>sale</u>. The <u>assistant showed</u> me the latest range of leather bags and <u>suitcases</u>. As I <u>travel</u> a lot I <u>always</u> need a <u>suitable collection</u> of bags and cases. The case needs <u>to</u> be sturdy, <u>lightweight</u> and strong. The hand <u>luggage</u> needs to be <u>flexible</u>, with many <u>compartments</u> and zipped <u>pockets</u>. Brown or <u>beige</u> is my <u>preferred</u> color. The <u>adjoining</u> store sold <u>perfume</u>, <u>which</u> I bought for my <u>niece</u>. I <u>decided</u> to go <u>to</u> the bookstore, picked up <u>several</u> <u>guidebooks</u> and <u>biographies</u>, then went to the checkout.

WORD SEARCH 1

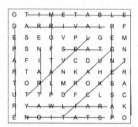

WORD LADDER 1

LINE; LANE; LAND; LEND; LEAD; READ

CONTINUOUS WORDS 1

Jeans Cornflower Indigo Iris Sapphire Eyes Denim Riband Glass Agapanthus Blueberry Turquoise Paint Shoes Uniform Crayon Bluebell Butterfly Aster Angelfish Shark Ribbon Pen Marker Fabric Delphinium Paper Ocean Flag Stamps Jay Sea Ink Sky Whale Dye Car Pufferfish Light Shirt Wool Lapis lazuli

WEB WORDS 1

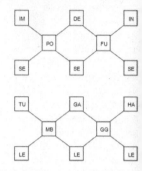

WORD CHAIN 1

There are many acceptable answers. Example:
COW HOW NOW NOT COT COO TOO TOE FOE FOR FOP LOP LOG LEG LAG HAG RAG RAT RAM RAN CAN CAT SAT SIT SET SEE BEE FEE GEE GET GOT
HEN PEN FEN FEW SEW SET SAT HAT HAM HEM HIM RIM RIP RAP SAP SAW SAY RAY LAY MAY MAT MAN MAR CAR FAR
PUT OUT CUT CUP CUR OUR OAR CAR FAR BAR BAN BAT BAG LAG LAW LAY PAY PAN PAT PAR PAW PEW YEW YET LET LIT LIP ZIP DIP DID DUD
ATE ARE ACE ICE IRE ORE ERE EVE EWE AWE AGE AGO EGO EGG
AIR SIR SIT SIN SIP RIP TIP LIP LIT PIT PIN PIG PIE LIE VIE VIM HIM HIT WIT BIT BAT BAN BAR BAG LAG LAX WAX

SOLVING SENTENCES 1
I WENT TO VISIT ADAM YESTERDAY BUT HE WAS ELSEWHERE. (The words have incorrect breaks)

TWISTER 1

TEN ADJECTIVES 1
There are many acceptable answers. Example:
Blue, bossy, big, bold, boring, beautiful, bashful, bendy, ballistic, balmy
Lonely, likeable, loveable, lovely, listless, lengthy, lumpy, little, limp, lively

FIRST LETTER 1
New letters: KAS
Word: ASK

PATTERNS 1
PATTERN: The words have the same vowel

SAM	KEN	JIM
KATH	JESS	GILL
PALM	YEW	FIR
HAT	VEST	SHIRT
BLACK	RED	PINK
LAMB	HEN	PIG

LETTER SQUARES 1
There are many acceptable answers. Example:
HAT - TOT - TEA - ASH
KITE - EAST - THIS - SINK
MAGIC - CAMEL - LIVER - REALM
DESERT - TIRADE - EVENTS - SPREAD

FICTIONAL LANGUAGE 1
It was the best thriller he had ever read and he could hardly put the AKLIBRO down. He turned the pages quickly, reading for hour after ORASKAPAN not even noticing when the clock chimed HATIGABI.

MISSING LETTERS 1
OBLIVIOUS, ACTIVATED

WORD TRAIL 2

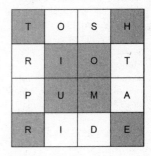

JOINING WORDS 2
TRA-IN-SERT; BO-AT-TEND; PLA-NE-ARLY; TRA-VEL-VET; HO-TEL-EVISE; TIC-KET-TLE; PASS-PORT-RAIT; BOO-KING-PIN; IS-LAND-ING

PYRAMID WORDS 2
There are many acceptable answers. Example:
A, AN, ANT, AUNT, AISLE, ALBEIT, ANGULAR, APTI-TUDE, ANSWERING, ARITHMETIC

LETTER CROSS 2
SODIUM

SPEED WORDS 2
There are many acceptable answers. Example:
Ant; Loathes; Manic; Vacant; Youthful; Divine; Igloo; Ooze; Mate; Zebra

WORKING IT OUT 2
Each word begins with one of the letters of the alphabet from A-Z

X WORDS 2

T	O	S	H
R	I	O	T
P	U	M	A
R	I	D	E

SYNONYMS 2
GRASS—LAWN; BUILDING—EDIFICE; DISEASE- AILMENT; INSTRUCTOR—EDUCATOR; COLLEAGUE -CO-WORKER; JOURNEY—VOYAGE; HINDRANCE— IMPEDIMENT; HERMIT—RECLUSE; FAMILY— KINSFOLK; SOLDIER—WARRIOR
SENTENCE: LOOK AFTER YOUR BRAIN

FIRST AND LAST LETTERS 2

There are many acceptable answers. Example:
COUNT, TACTIC, CHAT, TERRIFIC, CHIT, TOPIC, COURT, TIC, CLOUT, TRAGIC HINT, TOUCH, HIT, TORCH, HEAT, THOUGH, HEART, TOUGH, HAT, TROUGH EVEN, NOTE, EXPRESSION, NICE, EJECTION, NINE, ELATION, NERVE, EIGHTEEN, NURSE

SPLIT WORDS 2

CHIN; NECK; HEAD; HAND; CALF; FOOT; KNEE; NOSE

MEMORY GRID 2

1. BEAR; 2. HORSE; 2. MOOSE; 4. OX; 5. CAT

DEFINITIONS 2

Oblique: Slanting; **Squire:** Country gentleman; **Vapid:** Insipid, flat; **Scimitar:** Oriental curved sword; **Fez:** Conical red cap with tassel; **Bittern:** Marsh bird; **Conch:** Shellfish; **Meander:** Wander at random; **Nook:** Secluded corner; **Judder:** Shake noisily or violently

COLUMN WORDS 2

O	S	M	I	U	M
C	A	M	E	R	A
A	T	R	I	A	L
B	U	T	A	N	E
E	R	B	I	U	M
I	N	C	I	S	E

COMBINED ANAGRAMS 2

LION TIGER; MONKEY PIG; CAMEL WOLF

QUOTE GRID 2

QUOTE: THE PROBLEMS OF PUZZLES ARE VERY NEAR THE PROBLEMS OF LIFE, Erno Rubik
PHRASE: RUBIK'S MAGIC

WORD CAPSULE 2

There are many acceptable answers. Example:
CLASP; CHOSE; CREST; COBRA; CAROL; CHESS

MISSING ALPHABET 2

When Manuel knocked on the door he heard a growling sound. He jumped nervously, questioning why he was there. Could it be a grizzly bear? Anxiously he listened to the growls. He heard loud footsteps. The door was flung open and a tiny man looked up at him.

MINI WORD SUDOKU 2

E	T	O	H	M	D
D	M	H	E	T	O
M	E	D	T	O	H
H	O	T	D	E	M
O	D	E	M	H	T
T	H	M	O	D	E

WORDS FROM A WORD 2

There are many acceptable answers. Example:
Anemone
Useful, urgent
Socks, shoes, skirt
Tomato, tuna, toast, turkey
India, Idaho, Illinois, Iraq, Iceland
Norman, Neil, Nicholas, Nathan, Nando, Najib

RHYMING WORDS 2

ACHE, SQUAWK, CROAK, MONK, CHURCH, DREAD, HERD, CHIDE, NOD, FRAUD

NAMES 2

Boy's name	Extra letter
GEOFF	A
ISAAC	R
PETER	W
BORIS	E
CHRIS	N
OSCAR	D
ANDREW	

REMEMBERING NAMES AND FACES 2

From top to bottom: Frances; Henry; Scott; Nancy; Brenda; Terry.

CORRECTING SPELLING 2

My father is a great example of how life should be in retirement. He worked hard as a language teacher for almost forty years, and is now enjoying a fulfilling retirement. My dad has many hobbies; he has lots of friends, and he has looked after his health well by having many activities. His interests include various forms of dancing, calligraphy and philately (stamp collecting). He keeps in regular contact with all of his family, friends and acquaintances by phone or email. He is generous with his time and money, constantly willing to help others and do favors for them. He is also fun to be around as he is a great raconteur.

WORD SEARCH 2

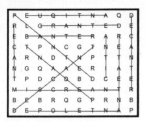

WORD LADDER 2

HAND; BAND; BEND; FEND; FEED; FEET

CONTINUOUS WORDS 2

Bluebird Meadowlark Godwit
Teal Tern Mockingbird Duck
Yellowhammer Kingfisher
Bustard Dabchick Kiwi Ibis
Cuckoo Osprey Falcon
Parakeet Robin Albatross
Saddleback Swift Oystercatcher
Tomtit Thrush Heron Ostrich
Vulture Rhea Goldfinch Hawk
Wren Cassowary Grebe
Cormorant Shoebill Flamingo
Quail Condor Eagle Pelican
Crane Emu Rail Plover Petrel
Lapwing Gull Finch

WEB WORDS 2

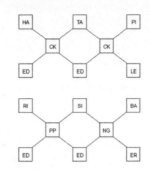

WORD CHAIN 2

There are many acceptable answers. Example:
TAN TIN TIE PIE PIN PIT PAT
PAN PAR CAR CAT CAN CON
COT HOT HAT HIT BIT BAT
BAN BAR FAR FAT FIT SIT
SIN SIR SIP TIP TAP TOP HOP
LOP LOT LOW SOW
SEE BEE BET LET SET SEA
PEA PEN PET PAT HAT HAM
DAM DAY SAY RAY LAY BAY
BAN BAR CAR TAR TAN TAP
TIP TIE LIE LIP HIP
TOO TON TOW COW COT
CAT HAT BAT BIT BET
SET MET MEN PEN DEN FEN
FEW SEW SOW COW HOW
NOW MOW BOW BOG LOG
LEG PEG BEG BEE BYE RYE
ROE TOE TOP
ILL ALL AIL AIR FIR FIN FIT
PIT HIT SIT LIT LIE PIE PIG
PEG LEG LOG LUG BUG BUT
BUN BAN VAN CAN CAR TAR
FAR PAR PAN PAD LAD LID
HID HIP SIP SIN PIN BIN
PAY RAY SAY LAY MAY MAN
MEN MET SET LET LEG PEG
PET PIT PIN PAN RAN RAG
BAG LAG SAG SAY WAY BAY
BAR BAT FAT HAT EAT EAR
WAR WAX TAX

SOLVING SENTENCES 2

SOMALIA IS ON THE EQUATOR AS IS KENYA AND UGANDA (The words and sentence are written backwards)

TWISTER 2

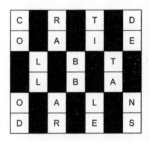

TEN ADJECTIVES 2

There are many acceptable answers. Example: Childish, cheerful, charming, cool, careful, cute, clever, considerate, clumsy, coastal
Great, glorious, gentle, gigantic, green, garish, golden, geeky, gorgeous, gallant

FIRST LETTER 2

New letters: WOC
Word: COW

PATTERNS 2

PATTERN: The words have the same number of letters

ALAN	JAMES	JOSEPH
ANNE	MARIA	JANICE
OHIO	TEXAS	ALASKA
BLUE	GREEN	PURPLE
MEAT	BREAD	CHEESE
GOLF	CHESS	SKIING

LETTER SQUARES 2

There are many acceptable answers. Example:
TOP - PEA - ARM - MAT
PRAY - YEAR - ROAD - DROP
KNAVE - ELECT - TOAST - TRICK
LOVING - GARAGE - ECZEMA - AMORAL

FICTIONAL LANGUAGE 2

Kelly loved going to the SINESAFIL especially on SABSEIJ nights with her friends. They would buy their tickets and some PAPMAI and settle down to watch the film.

MISSING LETTERS 2

BRUSQUELY, ANTIQUITY

WORD TRAIL 3

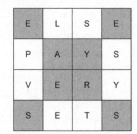

JOINING WORDS 3

LUP-IN-SIDE; PYL-ON-ION; THRE-AT-TEND; CAR-PET-AL; FRI-END-ING; MOT-HER-RING; STU-DENT-IST; INTE-REST-FUL; UNDER-HAND-SOME

PYRAMID WORDS 3

There are many acceptable answers. Example:
A, BY, CAN, DIET, EVENT, FATHOM, GUARDED, HEADACHE, INSTITUTE, JUGGERNAUT

LETTER CROSS 3

LAWYER

SPEED WORDS 3

There are many acceptable answers. Example:
You; Agree; Orange; Scoop; Abbots; Tricky; Quiet; Assess; Royal; Lower

WORKING IT OUT 3

All the letters are from the second half of the alphabet

X WORDS 3

E	L	S	E
P	A	Y	S
V	E	R	Y
S	E	T	S

SYNONYMS 3

DAWN-SUNRISE; SEAT-CHAIR; HOUSE-HOME; INSECT-BUG; THIEF-ROBBER; CLOTH-MATERIAL; PERSON-HUMAN; PARCEL-PACKET; SPEECH-PRESENTATION; FOG-MIST
SENTENCE: USE FIVE MINUTES WELL

FIRST AND LAST LETTERS 3

There are many acceptable answers. Example: SOUP, PRESS, SOAP, PASS, SHOP, PRICELESS, STOP, POINTLESS, STOOP, PLUS
RACING GEAR, RING, GLOW ER, RANG, GANDER, ROWING, GARDENER, RUNG, GARNER MAIL, LYCEUM, MEAL, LOOM, MEDAL, LOCUM, METAL, LOGARITHM, MENIAL, LISSOM

SPLIT WORDS 3

RICE; CAKE; TART; PEAR; PLUM; PORK; BEEF; VEAL

MEMORY GRID 3

1 .GUITAR; 2. SAXOPHONE; 3. HORN; 4. CELLO; 5. FLUTE

DEFINITIONS 3

Phoenix: A mythical bird burned in a funeral pyre, born again from the ashes; **Rejoinder:** A quick or witty reply; **Swarthy:** Having a dark skin; **Triathlon:** An athletic contest involving three events; **Weevil:** Small beetle with a long snout; **Liana:** A climbing plant that hangs from trees in tropical forests; **Serge:** Hard wearing woollen fabric; **Quark:** Group of subatomic particles; **Histrionic:** Excessively dramatic; **Importunate:** Very persistent

COLUMN WORDS 3

C	L	A	S	P	S
L	O	O	F	A	H
A	V	I	A	R	Y
B	I	L	L	E	T
U	N	D	O	N	E
I	G	N	I	T	E

COMBINED ANAGRAMS 3

ORANGE RED; BLUE BROWN; GRAY PURPLE

QUOTE GRID 3

QUOTE: I PERSONALLY BELIEVE WE DEVELOPED LANGUAGE BECAUSE OF OUR DEEP INNER NEED TO COMPLAIN, Jane Wagner
PHRASE: LANGUAGE SKILLS

WORD CAPSULE 3

There are many acceptable answers. Example:
TOTAL; TORSO; TOXIC; TIARA; TREAT; TENSE

MISSING ALPHABET 3

Manuel looked down at the tiny man. He was wearing enormous hobnailed boots. He also had a very strange expression on his face. "Hello" squeaked Manuel timidly. "I just wanted to ask if you have a grizzly bear in your apartment?" he added feeling embarrassed. "Step inside" the tiny man commanded.

MINI WORD SUDOKU 3

H	A	P	E	S	R
R	S	E	A	H	P
A	P	S	R	E	H
E	R	H	P	A	S
P	H	A	S	R	E
S	E	R	H	P	A

WORDS FROM A WORD 3

There are many acceptable answers. Example:
Magenta
Apple, artichoke
Duck, dog, dingo
Redford, Redgrave, Rogers, Robbins Iris, Irene, Imogen, Isobel, Ingrid Dancing, drawing, designing, driving, drumming, doodling

RHYMING WORDS 3

NEIGH, HARE, KNEE, FIEND, CHOIR, JUTE, FOE, SOUR, WAND, TRUE

NAMES 3

Girl's name	Extra letter
CAROL	S
POLLY	E
DIANE	H
HAZEL	I
SOFIA	A
GRACE	L
SHEILA	

REMEMBERING NAMES AND FACES 3

From top to bottom: Mike; Dave; Ted; Sue; Kate; Lynn

CORRECTING SPELLING 3

Maria had been reading a horror story about a woman in a foreign country who had been attacked by an amateur criminal. Strange and weird occurrences had been happening to the woman and she felt harassed and scared. Thunder and lightning seemed to be a regular weather pattern, making the electrical equipment malfunction. She heard frightening laughter coming from the next apartment, and was sure she spied another man carrying a knife. She seized the vegetable cutter, grateful that it had been sharpened, and peeped out of the window. There was definitely a second man.

WORD SEARCH 3

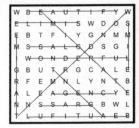

WORD LADDER 3

SAIL; SOIL; COIL; COAL; COAT; BOAT

CONTINUOUS WORDS 3

Potato Okra Artichoke Endive Celeriac Corn Brussels sprouts Spinach Kohlrabi Lentils Leek Kale Lettuce Calabrese Celery Yam Mushroom Mangetout Taro Onion Navy beans Shallot Turnip Pinto beans Pumpkin Turnip Parsnip Red pepper Rutabaga Asparagus Radicchio Bok choy Broccoli Cauliflower Radish Butternut squash Zucchini Garlic Chard Carrot Eggplant Wasabi Jerusalem artichoke Peas Cabbage Cucumber Chickpeas Alfalfa Black-eyed peas

WEB WORDS 3

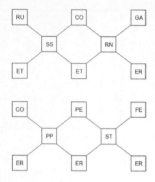

WORD CHAIN 3

There are many acceptable answers. Example:
SILL TILL TELL BELL BELT
MELT MALT MALE PALE PACE
LACE RACE RACK LACK
TACK SACK HACK BACK
BARK PARK LARK MARK
MASK BASK
DARE DATE LATE LATH BATH
PATH PATE RATE RITE ROTE
DOTE DOVE COVE CORE
WORE WERE WIRE FIRE
SIRE MIRE MORE LORE
CODE CORE CARE CASE
CAPE NAPE NAVE HAVE
HATE LATE MATE MITE RITE
RISE ROSE POSE PORE
PORK POCK LOCK SOCK
ROCK RACK PACK
WORD WORK FORK FORE
CORE BORE BORN TORN
TORE TIRE SIRE SURE PURE
PARE PANE PATE PACE LACE
LICE MICE MINE MIND MEND
BEND BENT
MUST DUST BUST BEST
BEAT BEAN BEAR DEAR
DEAN DEAL MEAL MEAT
SEAT SLAT SLAY PLAY CLAY
CLAP CLIP BLIP FLIP FLOP

SOLVING SENTENCES 3

SOME PEOPLE ARE HIGHLY
INTELLIGENT AND ARE ABLE
TO WORK OUT THESE KINDS
OF PUZZLES WITH LITTLE
DIFFICULTY (The words and
sentence are written backwards
with incorrect breaks)

TWISTER 3

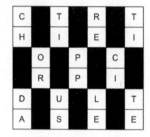

TEN ADJECTIVES 3

There are many acceptable
answers. Example: Hearty,
healthy, heavenly, huge,
hateful, handsome, heroic,
handy, hopeful, heavy
Tremendous, terrible, tortuous,
tiny, tender, tuneful, thick, thin,
thirsty, tidy
Virtual, viscous, violent,
verbose, vain, vacant, vague,
valiant, vivacious, vacuous

FIRST LETTER 3

New letters: YOJ
Word: JOY

PATTERNS 3

PATTERN: The words have the
same number of syllables

PAM	SUSAN	CHRISTINA
GEORGE	FRANKLIN	TIMOTHY
DOG	LION	ELEPHANT
SPAIN	HOLLAND	ITALY
LIME	ORANGE	BANANA
DUNE	STAR	LION KING

LETTER SQUARES 3

There are many acceptable
answers. Example:
WEED - DIGS - SAGA - ANEW
CURLY - YACHT - TOXIC -
CIVIC
HEALTH - HIATUS - SUBURB -
BLEACH FEATHER -
REALISM - MEMENTO -
ONESELF

FICTIONAL LANGUAGE 3

Little Tommy's dream was
to get a SERYETRA set for
his birthday. A big one with
PULACRI carriages. He lay
in bed at night making a
NAISDRE that it would come
true.

MISSING LETTERS 3

CUSTODIAN, CROSSWORD,
FACSIMILE

WORD TRAIL 4

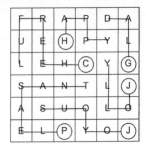

X WORDS 4

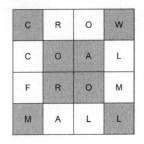

DEFINITIONS 4

Homage: Dutiful reverence;
Cursory: Hasty, hurried;
Risible: Laughable, ludicrous;
Paucity: Smallness of quantity;
Laconic: Brief, concise; **Sylph:**
Slender, graceful woman;
Pestle: Instrument for pounding
substances; **Cosmos:** The
universe as an ordered whole;
Quadriceps: Four-headed
muscle at front of thigh;
Topiary: Clipping shrubs into
ornamental shapes

JOINING WORDS 4

BAK-ER-MINE; HAND-LE-
SSON; AM-EN-TRY; GLO-
BAL-ANCE; CLO-SET-TLE;
FAL-CON-CERT; HALL- MARK-
SMAN; RAIN-FALL-IBLE; ANI-
SEED-LING

PYRAMID WORDS 4

There are many acceptable
answers. Example:
LA, EBB, ECHO, ADOPT,
BELIEF, AFFIXED, AGREE
ING, SHAPELESS,
MINIMIZING

LETTER CROSS 4

FRENCH

SPEED WORDS 4

There are many acceptable
answers. Example:
Lemon; Heaven; Wallow;
Possess; Church; Awry;
Interrupt; Questioning; Moose;
Chic

WORKING IT OUT 4

The words in each phrase have
1, 2, 3 and 4 syllables.

SYNONYMS 4

SAILOR-MARINER;
PROSPERITY—SUCCESS;
VALET—SERVANT;
NOVICE—BEGINNER;
SALARY— WAGES; ARMY—
TROOPS; DEPOSITORY—
WAREHOUSE; DELUGE—
FLOOD; GAIETY— JOLLITY;
AROMA—FRAGRANCE;
SENTENCE: IMPROVE YOUR
MEMORY DAILY

FIRST AND LAST LETTERS 4

There are many acceptable
answers. Example:
EXIT, TILE, EVENT, TIRE,
ELECT, TAKE, EIGHT, TRACE,
EJECT, TELEVISE
SHOAL, LASS, SCHOOL,
LOVELESS, SILL, LISTLESS,
SPILL, LOSS, SPOIL, LITMUS
PIER, RAMP, PEAR, RASP,
POOR, RUMP, PRAYER,
RECOUP, PEER, REVAMP

SPLIT WORDS 4

MILK; WINE; COLA; MEAD;
PORT; SODA; OUZO; BEER

MEMORY GRID 4

1. JAVELIN; 2. GOLF;
3. CYCLING; 4. DISCUS;
5. SKIING; 6. ROWING

COLUMN WORDS 4

S	T	R	E	E	T
T	W	I	R	L	S
T	E	N	D	E	R
A	L	C	O	V	E
E	V	O	K	E	D
D	E	P	E	N	D

COMBINED ANAGRAMS 4

EYE MOUTH; BROW CHIN;
CHEEK NOSE

QUOTE GRID 4

QUOTE: I'VE SAID TO MY
COACH THAT IF I'M FIT, I
THINK I CAN DO WELL, Usain
Bolt PHRASE: THE OLYMPIC
GAMES

WORD CAPSULE 4

There are many acceptable
answers. Example:
LILAC; LLAMA; LEMUR;
LEAST; LIMBO; LEARN

MISSING ALPHABET 4

The tiny man's apartment was full of exotic items and stuffed animals. Huge animals, such as jaguars, elephants, kangaroos and buffaloes. "Crazy" said Manuel quietly to himself, "very unexpected."

MINI WORD SUDOKU 4

R	E	K	N	O	C
O	C	N	R	K	E
C	K	O	E	R	N
N	R	E	O	C	K
K	N	R	C	E	O
E	O	C	K	N	R

WORDS FROM A WORD 4

There are many acceptable answers. Example:
Neck
Archery, athletics
Painting, pruning, playing
Lucid, lovely, legal, listless
Elephant, emu, elk, eagle, eel
Spain, San Diego, Switzerland, Stockholm, Sweden,
San Francisco

RHYMING WORDS 4

SUCCOR, SUEDE, SAID, SKILLED, AISLE, FOAL, FEIGN, BRAWN, YOUNG, HOARSE

NAMES 4

Boy's name	Extra let-
DAVID	S
CECIL	N
DEREK	T
COLIN	E
KEITH	V
LLOYD	E
STEVEN	

REMEMBERING NAMES AND FACES 4

From top to bottom: Robert; James; Jacinta; Sancho; Mary; Isabel

CORRECTING SPELLING 4

Vernon needed to find the questionnaire, and frantically searched in the stationery cupboard. Perseverance wasn't his strength and he was embarrassed by the number of documents he'd received and misplaced. On three separate occurrences he'd lost clients' subpoenas, though had immediately informed his supervisors in case they proceeded to inform the personnel department. He didn't want to be publicly shamed, have his office accommodation removed and be superseded by a junior lawyer.

WORD SEARCH 4

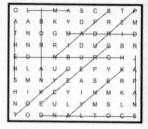

WORD LADDER 4

WELL; FELL; FEEL; FEET; FRET; FREE

CONTINUOUS WORDS 4

Kabul Algiers Canberra Vienna Nassau Brussels Sarajevo Gaborone Brasilia Sofia Rangoon Phnom Penh Beijing Zagreb Havana Nicosia Prague Copenhagen Djibouti Cairo London Addis Ababa Suva Helsinki Paris Tbilisi Berlin Accra Athens Nuuk Georgetown Budapest Reykjavik New Delhi Jakarta Teheran Baghdad Dublin Jerusalem Rome Kingston Tokyo Amman Nairobi Seoul Beirut Monrovia Tripoli Kuala Lumpur Rabat

WEB WORDS 4

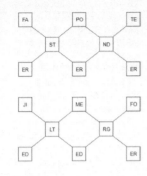

WORD CHAIN 4

There are many acceptable answers. Example:
FEAR BEAR BOAR BOAT COAT MOAT MEAT FEAT TEAT TENT WENT SENT SEND LEND LENT LINT LINE FINE FIND FUND FUNK PUNK PUNY
HINT MINT MINE TINE TINT TENT SENT SEND MEND BEND BENT DENT WENT WEND WIND RIND RINK SINK SUNK SANK RANK RACK SACK TACK
WILY WILL SILL SELL DELL DULL CULL CALL WALL WELL FELL FEEL FEET MEET BEET BEER SEER LEER PEER PIER PIED PIES LIES TIES
HERO HERS HENS PENS PANS PINS BINS BUNS BANS CANS CATS COTS LOTS LOSS MOSS BOSS BASS BASE CASE CAST CASH RASH RUSH
CORN CORE CONE DONE BONE LONE LANE PANE PANT PINT MINT MINK LINK LICK PICK PINK WINK WINE SINE SING SANG SONG LONG LONE HONE

SOLVING SENTENCES 4

THIS IS CORRECT BUT ALL THE LETTERS HAVE BEEN DOUBLED (X2). (Each letter is doubled and has incorrect breaks)

TWISTER 4

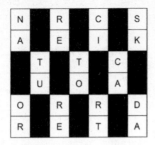

TEN ADJECTIVES 4

There are many acceptable answers. Example: Marvellous, mindful, mesmerising, meaty, melted, mean, magnificent, magical, misty, musical Open, overt, outstanding, ongoing, old, orange, old-fashioned, organised, obscure, occasional Pretty, plain, plentiful, plaintive, pertinent, pesky, pensive, pleated, pink, prim

FIRST LETTERS 4

New letters: NFA
Word: FAN

PATTERNS 4

PATTERN: The words have no double letters; one set of double letters and two sets of double letters

TROY	BARRY	RUSSSELL
BIANCA	SHEENA	COLLEEN
RODRIGUEZ	MATTHEWS	SMALLWOOD
COLORADO	HAWAII	MASSACHUSETTS
CLERK	ENGINEER	FOOTBALLER
CAKE	APPLE	TOFFEE

LETTER SQUARES 4

There are many acceptable answers. Example:
EAST - TIER - REST - TAKE HORSE - ENTRY - YIELD - DITCH SKIING - GARISH - HEARTH - HEARTS ELAPSES - SEVERAL - LITERAL - LICENCE

FICTIONAL LANGUAGE 4

Venn was nervous. Today was the athletics competition and he was entering the 100m PATURUFA. He wanted to MANALOFIR and bring home a GINTOOR medal to show his family and friends.

MISSING LETTERS 4

WAISTBAND, ATHEISTIC, NOSTALGIA

WORD TRAIL 5

BOA; CHAMELEON; IGUANA; LIZARD; PYTHON; TURTLE

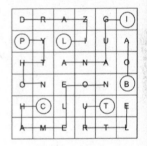

JOINING WORDS 5

SU-IT-EM; CO-AT-TIC; VE-ST-EAM; JUM-PER-PLEX; JAC-KET-CHUP; BLO-USE-FUL; SWIM-SUIT-CASE; UNI-FORM-ATION; NECK-LACE-RATE

PYRAMID WORDS 5

There are many acceptable answers. Example:
BE, SEE, DATE, LEAVE, STRIVE, BELIEVE, ADORABLE, IMMEDIATE, EFFERVESCE

LETTER CROSS 5

FINGER

SPEED WORDS 5

There are many acceptable answers. Example:
Flask; Insipid; Logic; Intelligent; Venomous; Topic; Socialism; Indeterminate; Zealously ; Fanfare

WORKING IT OUT 5

Each word ends in one of the letters of the alphabet from A-Z

X WORDS 5

M	A	N	Y
R	I	O	T
R	U	N	E
R	U	S	E

SYNONYMS 5

REPAIR-MEND; HURT-INJURE; GIGGLE-LAUGH; SMILE-GRIN; YELL-SHOUT; GIVE-DONATE; FIND- LOCATE; BUY-PURCHASE; PULL-TUG; HIT-PUNCH SENTENCE: SOLVING PROBLEMS IS EASY

FIRST AND LAST LETTERS 5

There are many acceptable answers. Example:
DIET, TEND, DENT, TREND, DOUBT, TIRED,
DISTANT, THIRD, DRAFT, TROD
NEVER, RAN, NEAR, RUN, NEWER, REMAIN,
NEARER, REGAIN, NEATER, RETAIN,GLASS, SING,
GROSS, SANG, GRASS, SLING, GAS,

SPLIT WORDS 5

FRANCE; JORDAN; TURKEY; POLAND; RUSSIA

MEMORY GRID 5

1. FOOT; 2. ARM; 3. NECK;
4. ONE; 5. TWO;
HAND, HEAD, HIP

DEFINITIONS 5

Cacophony: A mixture of loud and unpleasant sounds; **Kerfuffle:** A commotion; **Fricassee:** A dish of stewed meat in a thick white sauce; **Phalanger:** A tree dwelling marsupial; **Ruche:** A frill or pleat of fabric; **Xenophobia:** A strong dislike or fear of people from other countries; **Zealot:** A person who follows a cause very strictly; **Attar:** A sweet selling oil made of rose petals; **Edifice:** A large impressive building; **Ignominy:** Public disgrace

COLUMN WORDS 5

S	P	R	A	W	L
M	E	M	O	R	Y
E	N	T	A	I	L
S	C	O	U	T	S
B	I	T	T	E	R
A	L	M	O	S	T

COMBINED ANAGRAMS 5

BIG SMALL; SHORT TALL; FAT THIN

QUOTE GRID 5

QUOTE: IT IS THE MOST BIZARRE CONSPIRACY IN THE HISTORY OF THE WORLD, IT WILL COME OUT AT A FUTURE DATE, Jack Ruby
PHRASE: KENNEDY ASSASSINATION

WORD CAPSULE 5

There are many acceptable answers. Example:
BEAST; BENCH; BAKER; BRIDE; BALSA; BOAST

MISSING ALPHABET 5

"I'm professor Farquhar, taxidermist ... and slightly deaf" said the tiny man. "Would you like to join me in watching television?" Manuel felt hesitant. "I'm watching a documentary on grizzly bears. I need to listen with the sound turned up" he explained.

MINI WORD SUDOKU 5

I	N	G	E	A	M
E	M	A	I	N	G
N	A	I	G	M	E
G	E	M	N	I	A
M	G	N	A	E	I
A	I	E	M	G	N

WORDS FROM A WORD 5

There are many acceptable answers. Example:
Willow
Arm, ankle
Rhinoceros, robin, rat
Strawberry, sandwich, sausage, sprouts
Architect, artist, actor, art dealer, archivist William, Wesley, Wilson, Wade, Walter, Wilfred

RHYMING WORDS 5

SPRUCE, BLITZ, KOHL, TULLE, GROSS, LAPSE, CRECHE, FREIGHT, SWAT, SOUGHT

NAMES 5

Girl's name	Extra letter
WENDY	J
JANET	U
KYLIE	T
LAURA	E
SARAH	L
JOYCE	I
JULIET	

WORD SEARCH 5

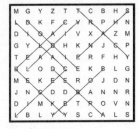

WEB WORDS 5

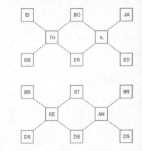

REMEMBERING NAMES AND FACES 5

From top to bottom: Michael; Leroy; Amy; Vida; Donald; Teresa.

CORRECTING SPELLING 5

It had been a beautiful wedding. Susan thought Tammy looked very glamorous in her bridal gown, but being her cousin, she was undoubtedly biased. Stephen the groom looked extremely handsome in his tuxedo, and the bridesmaids wore champagne-colored dresses and permanent smiles. They carried bouquets of pastel-hued freesias. Susan tried exceedingly hard not to cry as Tammy walked down the aisle and then declared her lifelong commitment to her new husband; but most of her female relatives were trying to suppress their tears. Handkerchiefs were in abundance. The honeymoon was in the Caribbean for a fortnight in September, immediately after the wedding.

WORD LADDER 5

BEEF; BEES; BEGS; BOGS; BOWS; COWS

CONTINUOUS WORDS 5

loganberry strawberry damson mango mandarin tangerine cherry boysenberry banana apple guava apricot tamarillo orange fig gooseberry grapefruit cantaloupe pomegranate tamarind date pear grape feijoa lime blackberry mulberry papaya avocado tomato rhubarb lychee persimmon lemon kumquat watermelon kiwifruit clementine cranberry peach plum raspberry jackfruit currant pineapple quince

WORD CHAIN 5

There are many acceptable answers. Example:
CALL CELL BELL BALL BILL SILL SELL TELL TALL TALE TAME CAME CAMP RAMP DAMP DAME DIME DIRE TIRE TILE RILE PILE PILL PALL PELL PELT BELT MELT MALT MALE PALE
NOTE MOTE MORE PORE PORN CORN CORE CARE FARE PARE BARE HARE DARE DARN WARN WARS CARS CATS MATS PATS HATS HATE LATE RATE GATE SATE MATE MITE MILE RILE
NEST PEST REST TEST VEST VAST LAST LEST BEST BEET BEER DEER DEAR FEAR PEAR PEAT BEAT NEAT NEAR HEAR HEAD READ BEAD BEAN LEAN MEAN MEAT MOAT BOAT **CLOG** BLOG FLOG FLAG FLAY CLAY PLAY PRAY PREY DREY DREG DREW CREW CROW BROW BLOW GLOW SLOW SLOT BLOT PLOT PLOY CLOY CLOD CLAD CLAM
DEEP PEEP PEER BEER BEET BENT RENT DENT SENT TENT TEST LEST REST BEST BUST RUST DUST LUST MUST MIST MINT LINT HINT HIND HAND LAND BAND RAND SAND SANE LANE LAKE BAKE CAKE CARE FARE

SOLVING SENTENCES 5
NOW THE SENTENCE IS BACKWARDS (X2)
(Each letter is doubled, is written backwards and has incorrect breaks)

TWISTER 5

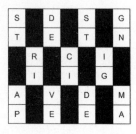

S		D		S		G
T		E		T		N
	R		C		I	
	I		I		G	
A		V		D		M
P		E		E		A

TEN ADJECTIVES 5
There are many acceptable answers. Example:
Fancy, flighty, fickle, fine, furious, fearsome, fearful, friendly, frightening, fat
Responsible, royal, red, respectable, reasonable, rosy, restful, resourceful, reliable, raging Slim, slender, shy, splendid, superb, superstitious, shameful, slight, sprightly, scandalous

FIRST LETTERS 5
New letters: EHT
Word: THE

PATTERNS 5
PATTERN: The words have the same middle letter

TRACY	SALLY	MARIA
SHANE	COLIN	GERRY
DRAKE	NOLAN	COREN
CRABS	MOLES	WORMS
PLAIN	FALSE	BORED
BEANS	MELON	CURRY

LETTER SQUARES 5
There are many acceptable answers. Example:
XENON - NOVEL - LILAC - CALYX
PENCIL - LOCKET - TOWING - GALLOP KESTREL - LITHIUM - MAMMOTH - HAMMOCK YACHTING - GRADIENT - THOUSAND - DAINTILY

FICTIONAL LANGUAGE 5
Flo loved her garden. Yellow flowers were her PINA- KITO and she particularly liked the beautiful laburnum PUNOJAU. Her prized plant was an orange HALAM- NAR followed by a sweet MABANSME rose.

MISSING LETTERS 5
CRINOLINE, AMPERSAND, PRINCIPLE, BRIEFCASE

WORD TRAIL 6
GIRAFFE; HORSE; LEOPARD; MONKEY; RABBIT; TIGER

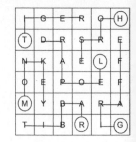

JOINING WORDS 6
FIN-AL-GAE; MAN-OR-BIT; POS-IT-CHY; MAS-COT-TAGE; NUM-BER-EFT; ITA-LIC-ENCE; MIS-SING-ULAR

PYRAMID WORDS 6
There are many acceptable answers. Example:
SO, SIT, STAY, STRAY, STRING, SPECIAL, SPELLING, SYNTHETIC, SYMPATHIZE

LETTER CROSS 6
BARLEY

SPEED WORDS 6
There are many acceptable answers. Example:
Yearly; Flow; Maniac; Digging; Eerie; Shockingly; Honest; Popular; Helicopter; Tenet

WORKING IT OUT 6
The words in each sentence are 1 to 8 letters long.

X WORDS 6

S	I	N	G	S
F	L	O	W	S
S	H	I	R	T
A	N	O	D	E
G	L	A	D	E

DEFINITIONS 6

Meteoric: Of the atmosphere; **Dorado:** Blue and silver sea fish; **Knell:** Sound of bell; **Virology:** Study of viruses; **Ylang ylang:** Malayan tree; **Omnivorous:** Feeding on many kinds of food; **Gung-ho:** Enthusiastic; **Circuitous:** Indirect, roundabout; **Leporine:** Of or like hares; **Wraith:** Person's apparition, ghost

MINI WORD SUDOKU 6

R	D	P	O	N	E
E	O	N	D	R	P
D	N	R	P	E	O
P	E	O	N	D	R
O	R	D	E	P	N
N	P	E	R	O	D

SYNONYMS 6

PROPHESY-FORETELL; CUDDLE-HUG; CUT-SLICE; EXTRICATE-DISENTANGLE; GAMBLE-BET; SCARE-FRIGHTEN; LESSEN-REDUCE; GLEAM-SHINE; TREMBLE-SHAKE; DECEIVE-DUPE SENTENCE: IMPROVE MEMORY AND RETENTION

COLUMN WORDS 6

A	S	S	I	S	T
S	T	R	U	T	S
P	I	L	L	O	W
A	C	T	I	N	G
S	K	E	W	E	R
A	S	S	E	S	S

WORDS FROM A WORD 6

There are many acceptable answers. Example:
Knee
Egypt, Ethiopia
Rifle shooting, rowing, rock climbing Alluringly, airily, awkwardly, angrily Lawyer, locksmith, lumberjack, lecturer, labourer Aardvark, antelope, anteater, asp, albatross, armadillo

FIRST AND LAST LETTERS 6

There are many acceptable answers. Example:
HEAL, LATH, HURL, LEECH, HOVEL, LURCH, HAIL, LUNCH, HURTFUL, LAUGH THING, GASH, TRYING, GLITCH, TOASTING, GIRTH, TUG, GNASH, TYPING, GUSH ROAD, DOUBTER, RENDERED, DEBTER, REBOUND, DEER, RESTED, DEAR, REWIND, DIVER

COMBINED ANAGRAMS 6

MOON SUN; BIRD PLANE; CLOUD STAR

QUOTE GRID 6

QUOTE: ALL WE HAVE TO DO IS PEEL THE SHRINES LIKE AN ONION, AND WE WILL BE WITH THE KING HIMSELF, Howard Carter PHRASE: THE TOMB OF TUTANKHAMUN

RHYMING WORDS 6

BRUISE, LORDS, COWS, DOZE, PAUSE, FIZZ, WISE, FREEZE, MAIZE, FOX

SPLIT WORDS 6

DONKEY; RABBIT; COUGAR; FERRET; JACKAL

WORD CAPSULE 6

There are many acceptable answers. Example:
ALIAS; AWASH; AFTER; ALONE; ALLOW; AMISS

NAMES 6

Boy's name	Extra letter
LEROY	G
HENRY	G
KEVIN	R
SIMON	O
JAMES	E
CHUCK	E
GEORGE	

MEMORY GRID 6

1. MEXICAN; 2. POLISH; 3. AUSTRALIAN; 4. JAPANESE; 5. CANADIAN; 6. ALGERIAN, KENYAN

MISSING ALPHABET 6

Tarquin could hardly believe his eyes. There, in the newspaper was the most amazing story he had ever read. JEALOUS HUSBAND CLAIMS WIFE IS IN LOVE WITH TAXI. "Good gracious ... in love with a taxi?" Tarquin asked himself, perplexed.

REMEMBERING NAMES AND FACES 6

From top to bottom: Louis; Jeremy; Rebecca; Carolyn; Bobby; Amanda

CORRECTING SPELLING 6

Johnny was four years old and his mother and father occasionally made an exception to his 7pm bedtime routine. This time they allowed him to stay up late to watch the opening ceremony of the Olympics as it promised to be a memorable occasion. He was fascinated and watched with great interest, often interrupting to ask pertinent questions. His mother explained that at the subsequent the Olympics he would be eight years old. Later, they were all feeling exhausted, and went to bed. The following morning Johnny's parents were looking at the Olympic sports schedule: decathlon, fencing, canoeing. Johnny looked at the television, observing that the Olympics were on again. Astonished, he turned to his mother and enquired "Am I eight now?"

WORD SEARCH 6

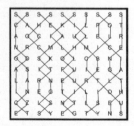

WORD LADDER 6

LOST; LIST; LINT; LINE; FINE; FIND

CONTINUOUS WORDS 6

Shocking Pink Khaki Ivory Yellow White Ecru Ultramarine Emerald Jade Amber Rust Taupe Cerise Scarlet Teal Lavender Red Burgundy Amethyst Navy Violet Burnt Orange Apricot Mustard Magenta Aquamarine Green Midnight Blue Auburn Azure Beige Gold Indigo Orange Olive Mauve Blue Peach Charcoal Lilac Cinnamon Brown Bronze Cream Crimson Maroon Magnolia Cyan Fuchsia Salmon Purple Periwinkle

WEB WORDS 6

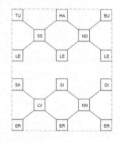

WORD CHAIN 6

HOPE ROPE ROVE RODE LODE MODE MADE MAKE RAKE CAKE LAKE SAKE SALE TALE BALE BAKE BIKE LIKE LINE LANE LAND RAND HAND HIND RIND RINK SINK SANK RANK

RISE RICE LICE LACE RACE RACK TACK TICK SICK SACK LACK BACK BECK PECK PACK PACE PARE CARE BARE BARN TARN TART PART PARK BARK LARK HARK HARE HATE

LAZY HAZY HAZE MAZE MATE MARE CARE PARE HARE HARD HAND WAND BAND BANK RANK RANG RING SING LING LONG

BACK RACK SACK TACK LACK LACE LICE RICE NICE MICE MACE FACE PACE PACK HACK HOCK LOCK DOCK MOCK SOCK SICK TICK

CREW

DREW DRAW DRAB CRAB CRIB DRIB DRIP TRIP TRAP TRAM CRAM CLAM CLAP CLAY CLOY PLOY PLOT PLOD

SOLVING SENTENCES 6

SAM EASES KIM OVER BRIDGE. HE ARRANGED EARLIER EVENTS. TOM ATE TEN TARTS AND A SALAD. (The words have incorrect breaks)

TWISTER 6

TEN ADJECTIVES 6

There are many acceptable answers. Example:
Delightful, dear, dreadful, deadly, dense, desirable, delicate, dastardly, dutiful, daring
Inspiring, insightful, interesting, icy, irascible, irritating,indescribable, illicit, insistent, intelligent
Nosey, nice, needy, numb, never-ending, noteworthy, nimble, nasty, noble, nefarious

FIRST LETTER 6

New letters: TVE
Word: VET

PATTERNS 6

PATTERN: The words have no vowel (AEIOU); one vowel or two vowels

LYNN	ANN	JEAN
GLYN	JOHN	NEIL
M^CFLY	BURNS	CLOUGH
GYPYSY	CLERK	COACH
GYM	CHESS	SQUASH
LYNX	PIG	DEER

LETTER SQUARES 6

There are many acceptable answers. Example:
DROOP - POWER - ROAST - TREND
GRUMPY - YELLOW - WHEELS - SAYING
WARBLED - DRESSER - REMINDS - SWALLOW
SOFTBALL - LONESOME - ENTERING - GIRAFFES

FICTIONAL LANGUAGE 6

Her son was LIMAQUI years old and loved posing challenging TANONDOX . "Mommy" he said "do stars fall out of the LANGITIEL and into the sea?" "No", she replied "why?" "Well where do starfish come from then?" he NAGTANQUE.

WORD TRAIL 7

BRAHMS; CHOPIN; DEBUSSY; DVORAK; ELGAR; HANDEL

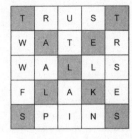

JOINING WORDS 7

WHA-LE-VER; LI-ON-CE; FR-OG-RE; WAL-RUS-SET; CH-IMP-ALE; CA-MEL-ODY; LEO-PARD-ON; FLAM-INGO-T

PYRAMID WORDS 7

There are many acceptable answers. Example:
BY, FLY, PLAY, HURRY, FLURRY, EMPATHY, MAHOGANY, GEOGRAPHY, PSYCHOLOGY

LETTER CROSS 7

VIOLET

SPEED WORDS 7

There are many acceptable answers. Example: Boarder; Tutu; Rhythm; Always; Quizzes; Zealot; Monitoring; Emerge; Liaison; Abbreviation

WORKING IT OUT 7

All the letters are from the first half of the alphabet

X WORDS 7

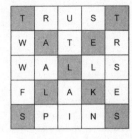

SYNONYMS 7

HATE-DETEST; ADMIT-CONFESS; ALLOW-PERMIT; ANNUAL-YEARLY; MIDDLE-CENTER; BEGIN-START; BLANK-EMPTY; OFTEN-FREQUENTLY; OLD-ANCIENT; BUSY-ACTIVE; ORAL-VERBAL; CHAMPION-WINNER
SENTENCE: WORD PUZZLES ARE EDUCATIONAL

FIRST AND LAST LETTERS 7

There are many acceptable answers. Example:
LAST, TOIL, LIST, TILL, LOST, TROLL, LINT, TALL, LEAST, TOOL
DRESS, SEND, DISTRESS, SAID, DAINTINESS, SLID, DECOMPRESS, SLED, DROWSINESS, SLAYED
HEAR, RICH, HOVER, RUSH, HOWEVER, RANCH, HOTTER, RASH, HEATER, REACH

SPLIT WORDS 7

BERLIN; LONDON; GENEVA; VENICE; FRESNO

MEMORY GRID 7

1. PATIENT, CARING;
2. ANIMATED, EXCITING;
3. DYNAMIC; 4. HAPPY, LIVELY; 5. PLEASANT;
6. PATIENT

DEFINITIONS 7

Clandestine: Kept secret; **Feverfew:** Plant with daisylike flowers; **Beatitude:** Very great happiness or blessedness; **Expatiate:** Speak or write at great length about; **Zephyr:** A soft gentle breeze; **Obdurate:** Stubbornly refusing to change ones mind; **Plangent:** Loud and mournful; **Radicchio:** Variety of chicory with dark red leaves; **Uvula:** Fleshy part of soft palate that hangs above the throat; **Saithe:** An edible North Atlantic fish

COLUMN WORDS 7

A	F	R	E	S	H
T	E	N	N	I	S
I	M	P	O	S	E
P	A	L	A	T	E
F	L	O	W	E	R
T	E	N	O	R	S

COMBINED ANAGRAMS 7

HAM PORK; BREAD TUNA; BEEF CHEESE; RICE CARROT

QUOTE GRID 7

QUOTE: EVERY TWO YEARS THE AMERICAN POLITICS INDUSTRY FILLS THE AIRWAVES WITH CHARACTER ASSASSINATIONS OF EVERY POLITICAL PRACTITIONER AND THEN DECLARES THAT AMERICA HAS LOST TRUST IN ITS POLITICIANS, Charles Krauthammer
PHRASE: AMERICAN PRESIDENTIAL ELECTION

WORD CAPSULE 7

There are many acceptable answers. Example: DRESS; DEBUT; DIVER; DINGO; DIVAN; DOING

MISSING ALPHABET 7

The man's wife was with her beloved taxi all day long. She cleaned, waxed and polished it lovingly, never questioning how strange it seemed. She failed to realize how rejected it could make a man feel.

MINI WORD SUDOKU 7

M	R	B	U	E	N
E	U	N	R	B	M
U	E	M	N	R	B
B	N	R	M	U	E
N	B	U	E	M	R
R	M	E	B	N	U

WORDS FROM A WORD 7

There are many acceptable answers. Example: Maori
Ostrich, oystercatcher
Silver, salmon, scarlet
Chest, calf, cheek, chin
Ottawa, Oslo, Oxford, Ontario, Osaka
Wriggle, walk, wrestle, waddle, whisper, whistle

RHYMING WORDS 7

ROSE, SQUEEZE, GAZE, LOCKS, STICKS, FLEX, AX, MOVE, GIVE, EVE

NAMES 7

Boy's name	Extra letter
BOBBY	A
JASON	T
BRIAN	R
LENNY	L
GRANT	E
DIEGO	W
WALTER	

REMEMBERING NAMES AND FACES 7

From top to bottom: Todd; Earl; Connie; Victor; Emily; Crystal

CORRECTING SPELLING 7

Gregory Harris was <u>having</u> a <u>challenging</u> day. <u>Being</u> <u>principal</u> of a <u>kindergarten</u> was a <u>prestigious</u> role, but a busy one. Sometimes he had to teach, <u>which</u> meant he had to constantly <u>develop</u> his <u>knowledge</u>. This week he gave <u>lessons</u> on <u>squirrels</u>, <u>ostriches</u> and penguins, and helped with <u>rehearsals</u> for the <u>upcoming</u> show. He <u>wondered</u> about the <u>feasibility</u> of <u>employing</u> <u>another</u> teacher but the figures <u>simply</u> didn't add up. <u>There</u> weren't <u>sufficient</u> funds. "Money, we <u>always</u> need money," he said to himself <u>forlornly</u>. "Mr Harris," said a <u>concerned</u> four-year- old, "<u>would</u> you like some of my <u>pocket</u> money?"

WORD SEARCH 7

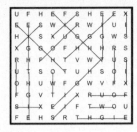

WEB WORDS 7

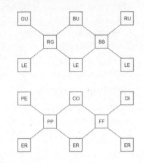

TWISTER 7

WORD LADDER 7
WARM; WART; CART; CAST; COST; COSY

CONTINUOUS WORDS 7
Grasshopper Kiwifruit Turtle Eyes Shamrock Kelp Parsley Zucchini Iguana Algae Elves Snake Emerald Grape Peridot Lettuce Cress Spinach Holly Kryptonite Fern Money Lizard Broccoli Jade Avocado Olive Celery Grass Spirulina Apple Peas Sprouts Chrysalis Caterpillar Pepper Clover Cactus Moss Mint Lime Artichoke Cucumber Marrow Frog Cabbage Asparagus Leaf Praying mantis

WORD CHAIN 7
There are many acceptable answers. Example:
MESH MASH CASH DASH RASH BASH HASH LASH LAST LOST LIST LUST RUST DUST MUST MAST FAST FIST FISH DISH WISH WASH
DRAG BRAG BRAT BRAN GRAN GRIN GRIP DRIP DROP CROP CROW BROW BREW BLEW BLOW GLOW FLOW FLAW FLAG
SNOW SHOW SHOT SLOT PLOT PLOY PLOP PROP DROP DRIP GRIP GRIM GRID GRIN GAIN LAIN MAIN RAIN VAIN VEIN REIN
FLEE FREE TREE THEE THEN THAN THIN CHIN CHIP SHIP SHOP CHOP CLOP CLAP CLAY FLAY FLAT FLAN CLAN CLAD
WORK CORK CORN CORE CARE HARE RARE PARE PART PORT PORK PORE MORE LORE SORE FORE FARE FAKE TAKE LAKE BAKE CAKE SAKE SALE TALE TILE RILE MILE

SOLVING SENTENCES 7
MEET YOUR TEAM NEIL. AVOID THEIR LOUD NOISY FEUD THOUGH, IT WEARS US OUT. (Each word contains an additional R in the middle)

TEN ADJECTIVES 7
There are many acceptable answers. Example:
Ardent, arresting, adventurous, ample, aggressive, ambient, anabolic, affable, awkward, airy Elegant, edgy, entertaining, effervescent, eager, educated, eligible, edible, eminent, erudite White, wan, willing, wishful, weighty, wealthy, woeful, wasteful, weeping, wobbly

FIRST LETTER 7
New letters: UDM Word: MUD

PATTERNS 7
PATTERN: The words end in the same letter

SEAN	MIKE	PHIL
JOAN	KATE	NELL
BROWN	WHITE	TEAL
DALMATION	POODLE	SPANIEL
HAWKMAN	HAWKEYE	HAWKGIRL
CYCLAMEN	ANEMONE	BLUEBELL

429

LETTER SQUARES 7

There are many acceptable answers. Example: GAUCHO - ORANGE - EXCESS - SEEING WEATHER - REMORSE - EXPIRES - SPARROW STARSHIP - POMANDER - RIVERBED - DEFTNESS NIGHTFALL - LUDICROUS - SOLICITOR - RADIATION

FICTIONAL LANGUAGE 7

It was the worst holiday they had ever been on! The hotel KUWARSAL was dirty, the beds were BUKOLUN and the windows wouldn't BUKASAB. The hotel staff who made breakfast even managed to burn the TUSTAGRIL.

WORD TRAIL 8

CABBAGE; CARROT; CORN; PUMPKIN; SPROUT; TURNIP

A	R	R	O	S	R
C	T	E	T	O	R
R	U	G	T	U	N
N	B	A	P	U	R
B	A	C	M	O	
P	N	I	K	C	

JOINING WORDS 8

PLACA-TE-NSION; LIV-ID-ENTIFY; TANGR-AM- POULE; ANAE-MIC-ROBE; MID-WAY-SIDE; TANK- ARD-UOUS; FE-MALE-VOLENT; HO-STEL-LAR; NAR-RATE-PAYER

PYRAMID WORDS 8

There are many acceptable answers. Example: BE, BAN, BAND, CIVIL, AVERSE, CUTLASS, CARELESS, ESSENTIAL, HOPELESSLY

LETTER CROSS 8

WALRUS

SPEED WORDS 8

There are many acceptable answers. Example: Congratulations; Rotator; Seethe; Hypothesis; Educated; Kissing; Backhand; Settles; Begin; Schools

WORKING IT OUT 8

Alternate words are palindromes.

X WORDS 8

F	O	L	I	C
C	O	U	R	T
P	L	O	Y	S
S	P	A	D	E
S	W	I	M	S

SYNONYMS 8

STERN-AUSTERE; USEFUL-BENEFICIAL; ENDED- TERMINATED; BRIEF-CONCISE; EXTRA-ADDITIONAL; SULKY-MOROSE; CONSPICUOUS-VISIBLE; WEIGHTY-HEAVY; WATCHFUL-ALERT; FRUGAL-MISERLY; JUSTIFIABLE-DEFENSIBLE; FAULTLESS-IMMACULATE SENTENCE: DO YOUR TRAINING DAILY

FIRST AND LAST LETTERS 8

There are many acceptable answers. Example:
GOAL, LEG, GAOL, LAG, GEL, LONG, GIRL, LOG, GILL, LOVING
RIOT, TEAR, REST, TRAINER, RANT, TILLER, RENT, TIER, REVERT, TAILOR
DEVIL, LAND, DEAL, LEAD, DENTAL, LACED, DRIVEL, LARD, DECAL, LUCID

SPLIT WORDS 8

YELLOW; VIOLET; SILVER; PURPLE; MAROON

MEMORY GRID 8

1. GARAGE; 2. PALACE; 3. GALLERY, THEATRE; ONE SPACE BELOW; 5. CABIN; 6. SIX: CASTLE, GARAGE, HOUSE, STORE, TEMPLE, PALACE

DEFINITIONS 8

Privation: Loss or absence; **Thither:** To that place; **Ingurgitate:** Swallow greedily; **Desalinate:** Remove salt from; **Noggin:** Small mug or measure; **Hoopoe:** Bird with variegated plumage; **Scilla:** Bulbous plant; **Vintner:** Wine merchant; **Ambiversion:** Balance between introversion and extroversion; **Kanaka:** Pacific islander

COLUMN WORDS 8

A	D	R	I	F	T
M	A	J	O	R	S
A	N	S	W	E	R
D	I	N	I	N	G
A	S	P	E	C	T
R	H	Y	T	H	M

STRINGS 8

There are many acceptable answers. Example: CANOPY, YOUNGSTER, RELIABLE, EVENTUAL, LOG

COMBINED ANAGRAMS 8

APPLE PLUM; ORANGE PEAR; GRAPE PEACH; APRICOT LEMON

QUOTE GRID 8

QUOTE: CHRISTMAS BEGINS ABOUT THE FIRST OF DECEMBER WITH AN OFFICE PARTY AND ENDS WHEN YOU FINALLY REALIZE WHAT YOU SPENT, AROUND APRIL FIFTEENTH THE NEXT YEAR, P.J. O'Rourke

PHRASE: CHRISTMAS PARTY CELEBRATIONS

WORD CAPSULE 8

There are many acceptable answers. Example: BLIMP; BIJOU; BOWER; BLEEP; BAGEL; BADGE

MISSING ALPHABET 8

The man felt so dejected and unquestionably angry that he sold his wife's prized taxi! "Perhaps I can use the sixteen thousand dollars to take my wife on vacation" he thought.

MINI WORD SUDOKU 8

I	S	G	L	A	N
N	A	L	I	G	S
G	N	A	S	I	L
L	I	S	A	N	G
S	G	I	N	L	A
A	L	N	G	S	I

WORDS FROM A WORD 8

There are many acceptable answers. Example: Newton
Aluminium, argon
Pleasure, panic, peacefulness
Ibis, ibex, iguana, impala
Eagerly, easily, earnestly, efficiently, extremely
Raspberry, rhubarb, risotto, radish, ragout, rice

RHYMING WORDS 8

TACKS, SLEEVE, HEATH, BERTH, GHOST, EAST,WORST, GUEST, LAST, WEPT

NAMES 8

Boy's name	Extra letter
PABLO	T
ETHAN	A
BRUCE	R
LEWIS	U
SHANE	H
CLINT	R
ARTHUR	

REMEMBERING NAMES AND FACES

From top to bottom: Wesley; Pedro; Vivienne; Roberta; Greg; Ida

CORRECTING SPELLING 8

Julie <u>decided</u> to <u>announce</u> that she was on a diet. Her <u>friends</u> <u>were impressed</u> and <u>would</u> help out when they could. They didn't <u>offer</u> her <u>cookies</u>, and only served black <u>coffee</u> when she came to <u>visit</u>. Julie liked the <u>attention</u>, and <u>would instantaneously</u> start <u>discussing</u> diets <u>whenever</u> she was with her <u>colleagues</u>. <u>Unfortunately</u> Julie worked in a canteen and was <u>surrounded</u> by food. <u>Temptation</u> was <u>everywhere</u>: <u>sandwiches</u>, <u>spaghetti</u> and <u>tomato</u> sauce, <u>pumpkin</u> pie, <u>rhubarb</u> crumble and <u>raspberry</u> <u>cheesecake</u>. She took food from the <u>trolley</u> and ate it in <u>secret</u>. Julie's boss was <u>observant</u> and <u>arranged</u> for her to move to a <u>different</u> department, one <u>where</u> <u>there</u> was no food.

WORD SEARCH 8

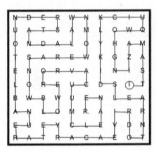

WORD LADDER 8

SING; SINE; DINE; DONE; DOTE; NOTE

CONTINUOUS WORDS 8

Armchair Radio Ottoman
Microwave Wastebasket
Table Ornament Linen Towels
Candlestick Cooker Recliner
Settee Shelf Futon Bureau
Couch Hammock Hamper
Refrigerator Bassinet Bookshelf
Television Carpet High-chair
Bench Chest Stool Lamp
Computer Sofabed Clock
Closet Sideboard Mattress Bowl
Bed Deckchair Cot Footstool
Plate Screen Dishwasher
Drapes Cupboard Desk Jug
Mirror Divan Writing Desk

WEB WORDS 8

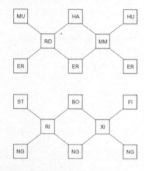

WORD CHAIN 8

There are many acceptable
answers. Example:
WAGER WAFER WATER LATER
LASER LOSER LOVER COVER
HOVER ROVER MOVER
MOVED LOVED LIVED LIVER
LIVEN LIVES WIVES
SEEMS SEEPS SEERS PEERS
PEARS TEARS TEATS MEATS
SEATS BEATS BELTS PELTS
PESTS VESTS RESTS
CALLS BALLS BELLS BILLS
SILLS SELLS PELLS PELTS
MELTS MEETS BEETS BEERS
BEARS BEAKS LEAKS LEANS
DEANS
BERRY FERRY FURRY CURRY
CARRY MARRY MERRY PERRY
PARRY TARRY HARRY HURRY
WIPER WIPES WIPED PIPED
PIPER PAPER PAGER WAGER
WADER WADED FADED FACED
LACED RACED

SOLVING SENTENCES 8

IS IT EASY TO READ THE
FIRST HALF ONE WAY, AND
THEN THE SECOND HALF
THE OTHER WAY ROUND?
(There are incorrect breaks. The
words in the second half are
written backwards)

TWISTER 8

TEN ADJECTIVES 8

There are many acceptable
answers. Example: Jovial, juicy,
judgemental, judicious, joyful,
joyous, just, jittery, jammy, jazzy
Knowledgeable, knowing,
kissable, kinky, keen, kind,
kindred, karmic, knitted, knotted
Underhand, untidy,
understanding, useful, usual,
uncoordinated, urgent,
unaccompanied, upbeat, ugly

FIRST LETTER 8

New letters: PZI
Word: ZIP

PATTERNS 8

PATTERN: The words have the
same vowels in the same order
within the word

KAREN	JENNI	TESSA
CALEB	DENNIS	DEAN
PARKER	ELLIS	BELLAMY
FRANCE	DELHI	ENGLAND
TRAVEL	SEWING	NETBALL
CAKE	HERRING	PEACH

LETTER SQUARES 8

There are many acceptable
answers. Example: MENTOR -
REMIND - DRINKS - SCHISM
CHERISH - HAULAGE -
ERRATIC - CHAOTIC
HEADACHE - EARLIEST -
TRUSTING - GHOULISH
EVERGREEN - NOISINESS -
SUMMARIZE - EMPHASIZE

FICTIONAL LANGUAGE 8

She loved going to watch
the dance competitions.
The women wore beautiful
MAGDAJUX the men looked
handsome, and she liked
listening to the lively HIMIMU.
She wished she had gone to
dance KLASELEA when she
was younger, but always felt
like she had two left PAAPIEX.

WORD TRAIL 9

COOKER; CUTLERY; KETTLE;
PLATE; REFRIGERATOR

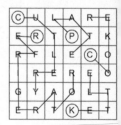

JOINING WORDS 9

COU-CH-EER; TAB-LE-MON; CLOS-ET-HER; DRA-PES-KY; CAR-PET-ITION; CH-AIR-PORT; ST-AIRS-TRIP; PAIN-TING-LE; PIC-TURE-EN

PYRAMID WORDS 9

There are many acceptable answers. Example: ZA, YES, XRAY, WHALE, VENDOR, UNUSUAL, THREATEN, SENSITIVE, REGIMENTED

LETTER CROSS 9

GUITAR

SPEED WORDS 9

There are many acceptable answers. Example: Psychology; Curious; Oxygen; Galore; Sheepish; Pontoon; Flesh; Civic; Toothpaste; Aura

WORKING IT OUT 9

Each sentence contains an anagram: SALESMEN NAMELESS; TEARDROP PREDATOR; RATTLES STARTLE; SECURED RESCUED; ARREST RAREST; TEASED SEDATE; HARDEST TRASHED.

X WORDS 9

P	R	O	N	G
M	E	R	R	Y
F	L	A	S	H
S	P	A	C	E
E	P	O	C	H

SYNONYMS 9

LOYAL-FAITHFUL; POLITE-COURTEOUS; REAL-GENUINE; RICH-WEALTHY; RUDE-IMPOLITE; SAD-UNHAPPY; SLEEPY-DROWSY; SLIM-SLENDER; USUAL-COMMON; WEAK-FEEBLE; WELL-KNOWN–FAMOUS; HIGH-TALL
SENTENCE: HELPING DISCIPLINE YOUR BRAIN

FIRST AND LAST LETTERS 9

There are many acceptable answers. Example: LEMON, NAVEL, LEAN, NAVAL, LOAN, NATAL, LESSEN, NAUTICAL, LESSON, NICKEL NODDING, GRIN, NURTURING, GAIN, NESTING, GROWN, NAGGING, GLEAN, NUMBING, GRAIN TEN, NEST, TIN, NEWT, TRAIN, NEAT, TOWN, NOT, THEN, NOUGHT

SPLIT WORDS 9

MINISTER; WAITRESS; MUSICIAN; SCULPTOR

MEMORY GRID 9

FIFTEEN; SIX;ELEVEN; TWENTY;EIGHT; THIRTY; FORTY THREE

DEFINITIONS 9

Rampart: A wall built to defend a castle; **Pachyderm:** A large animal with thick skin; **Ligature:** A cord used to tie up a bleeding artery; **Duiker:** African antelope; **Vermiform:** Having the form of a worm; **Yawl:** A sailing boat with two masts; **Mycology:** The scientific study of fungi; **Gesso:** A hard compound of plaster of Paris used in sculpture; **Morpheme:** The smallest unit of meaning that a word can be divided into; **Claymore:** A large type of sword used in Scotland

COLUMN WORDS 9

S	W	O	O	S	H
T	I	S	S	U	E
I	N	C	O	M	E
S	T	O	R	M	Y
S	E	L	L	E	R
E	R	R	O	R	S

STRINGS 9

There are many acceptable answers. Example: HONEY, YELLOW, WITNESS, SPECIAL, LEVER, RANGE

COMBINED ANAGRAMS 9

CRAB SEAL; WHALE SQUID; LOBSTER SHARK; OCTOPUS OYSTER

QUOTE GRID 9

QUOTE: NOTHING IS MORE CONTRARY TO THE ORGANIZATION OF THE MIND, OF THE MEMORY, OF THE IMAGINATION ... IT'S JUST TORMENTING THE PEOPLE WITH TRIVIA!, Napoleon I
PHRASE: ADVENT OF THE METRIC SYSTEM

WORD CAPSULE 9

There are many acceptable answers. Example: KETCH; KARMA; KNOWN; KNEAD; KNEEL; KNIFE WALTZ; WEAVE; WHELP; WATCH; WORRY; WAGER

MISSING ALPHABET 9

His wife was livid! She jumped and screamed like a crazy woman! "You get my taxi back instantly!" she squealed, hurling an ax at him ferociously.

MINI WORD SUDOKU 9

G	O	A	J	N	R
N	J	R	A	O	G
A	R	J	N	G	O
O	N	G	R	A	J
R	G	N	O	J	A
J	A	O	G	R	N

WORDS FROM A WORD 9

There are many acceptable answers. Example:
Quail
Urdu, Ukrainian Eye, ear, elbow
Beekeeper, builder, banker, baker
Excite, equate, ethics, elicit, eating
Carbon, cadmium, chlorine, cobalt, chromium, copper

RHYMING WORDS 9

WEST, BLUNT, CENT, FEINT, COLT, JILT, MELT, SECT, BOOT, SCOUT

NAMES 9

Girl's name	Extra letter
ALICE / CELIA	P
BETTY	L
DORIS	I
JACKY	N
ELLEN	U
VICKY	E
TRUDY	A
PAULINE	

REMEMBERING NAMES AND FACES 9

From top to bottom: Ethel; Raul; Ryan; Georgia; Angel; Jackie; Constance; Brett

CORRECTING SPELLING 9

Carlos looked at the <u>calendar</u> and started to <u>panic</u>. <u>Tomorrow</u> was the <u>twelfth</u>, his wedding <u>anniversary</u>, and he had <u>forgotten</u>! He would <u>definitely</u> be in <u>trouble</u> if he <u>merely</u> gave his wife a card. A big <u>argument</u> would be a <u>certainty</u>. Carlos found he could <u>excel</u> at times like this. He could <u>usually</u> <u>devise</u> a <u>successful</u> solution. Quickly he called a <u>restaurant</u>, one with a <u>foreign</u> name, <u>which</u> he <u>believed</u> sounded more romantic. He booked a pink <u>me-tallic</u> <u>limousine</u> and <u>ordered</u> lilac <u>fuchsias</u>. <u>Their</u> evening was a <u>genuine</u> <u>success</u>. "Thanks for a <u>terrific</u> time" said his wife "<u>you're</u> <u>great</u> at planning <u>surprises</u> in advance."

WORD SEARCH 9

WORD LADDER 9

TIPQ; TMPQ; TMJQ; TMJE; TBJE; SBJE
Code: Take the preceding letter in the alphabet. SHOP, SLOP, SLIP, SLID, SAID, RAID

CONTINUOUS WORDS 9

Coccyx Annex Flex Excel Except Anorexia Convex Vixen Intoxicated Detox Oxide Elixir Relax Apex Galaxy Sixteen Next Tuxedo Onyx Luxury Influx Index Exempt Text Waxy Vortex Exams Fixate Toxic Calix Exciting Crucifix Exit Oxtail Lexicon Oxygen Existing Foxglove Roux Proxy Syntax Hexagon Thorax Hoax Xenophobia Approximate Extend Dextrous Sphinx Matrix Prefix Taxi Pixies Peroxide Export Paradox Boxing Coaxed Mixture Maxim

WEB WORDS 9

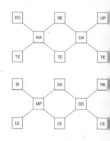

WORD CHAIN 9

There are many acceptable answers. Example: **THINK**
THINE SHINE SHONE SHORE SHORN SCORN SCORE STORE STONE STOKE STAKE SNAKE SNARE
COULD WOULD WOUND ROUND POUND SOUND FOUND HOUND MOUND MOUNT
PLEAS FLEAS FLEES FREES TREES TRESS DRESS DREGS DRAGS BRAGS BRATS BRASS GRASS GRABS GRUBS
NEVER NEWER FEWER FEVER LEVER SEVER SEWER SOWER ROWER COWER COWED ROWED BOWED BORED BOXED BODED **SCARE** SCORE SWORE STORE STOVE STAVE SLAVE SHAVE SHAKE SHARE SHAPE SHADE

SOLVING SENTENCES 9

WE STOP ONE CAR, BERYL, BUT DON'T SAVE TIME, TIM. (The words are written backwards and have incorrect breaks)

TWISTER 9

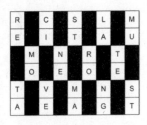

TEN ADJECTIVES 9

There are many acceptable answers. Example: Quarrelsome, quarterly, quick, queer, quizzical, quivery, quaky, questionable, quotable, quirky Young, youthful, yellow, yappy, yearly, yummy, yucky, yeasty, yodelling, yearling

FIRST LETTER 9

New letters: BGLI
Word: GLIB

PATTERNS 9

PATTERN: The first word begins and ends with the same letter; the second word ends with the next letter of the alphabet; the third word ends with the next-but-one letter of the alphabet

ANNA	DIANE	KIM
BOB	HENRI	LEON
NORTHAMP-	MILTON	LINCOLN
GARDENING	FARMING	ENGINEERING
REINDEER	DOVE	JACKAL
URDU	HINDI	FRENCH

LETTER SQUARES 9

There are many acceptable answers. Example: RONDEAU - UKELELE - EAGERLY - YOUNGER ELEPHANT - TORTOISE - ELEVATES - STOPPAGE ALGORITHM - MUSKETEER - REFURBISH - HYPERBOLA HEADMASTER - RETREATING - GRATUITOUS - SEVENTIETH

FICTIONAL LANGUAGE 9

It was his first trip to APRUGA and he was enjoying the MAINCHAU weather. The river looked beautiful and he decided to go on a BANGKABAT trip. It wasn't safe to swim in the river as there were BUWAYAX basking at the water's edge, but he got out his camera and took plenty of LITRATOX.

WORD TRAIL 10

CIRCLE; OBLONG; OVAL; SPIRAL; SQUARE; TRIANGLE

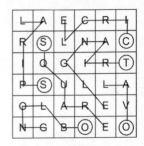

JOINING WORDS 10

RAN-CH-EESE; SCA-LY-RIC; MON-EY-ELASH; TURKEY-RING; US-HER-MIT; ZEA-LOT-US; PE-TREL-LIS; TH-WART-HOG; W-RECK-ON

PYRAMID WORDS 10

There are many acceptable answers. Example: RE, SEE, THEN, USING, VALUED, WILLING, XEROXING, YOUNGSTER, ZYGOMORPHY

LETTER CROSS 10

THAMES

SPEED WORDS 10

There are many acceptable answers. Example: Manifesto; Role; Ingesting; Kamikaze; Lime; Unavoidably; Perish; Martial; Systemic; Withhold

WORKING IT OUT 10

All the words are 3, 4 and 5 letters long

X WORDS 10

B	E	L	O	W
M	E	S	H	Y
S	W	I	L	L
S	T	A	G	E
E	L	A	T	E

SYNONYMS 10

IMMINENT-IMPENDING;
EXORBITANT-EXCESSIVE;
EXTENSIVE-WIDESPREAD;
MERCIFUL-CLEMENT;
OBVIOUS-UNMISTAKABLE;
HABITUAL-CUSTOMARY;
EMPOWERED-AUTHORIZED;
FLORID-FLUSHED;
MALEVOLENT-MALICIOUS;
TEMPTING-ENTICING;
OPPORTUNE-FAVORABLE;
GULLIBLE-NAIVE
SENTENCE: COMPLETE THE
FUN CHALLENGES

FIRST AND LAST LETTERS 10

There are many acceptable
answers. Example: EGRESS,
SENSE, EASINESS, SIZE,
EFFORTLESS, SLAVE,
EAGERNESS, STOVE,
ENDLESS, STONE ARM,
MANIA, ALARM, MALARIA,
ANTHEM, MEDIA, AFFIRM,
MANTRA, ALBUM, MARINA
COAL, LILAC, COOL, LACTIC,
CRAWL, LACONIC, CHILL,
LIMBIC, CAROL, LOGIC

SPLIT WORDS 10

SQUIRREL; KANGAROO;
ANTELOPE; HEDGEHOG

MEMORY GRID 10

1. AT THE BOTTOM OF THE
GRID; 2. RIGHT;
3. UP, ABOVE; 4. BESIDE;
5. THREE: BESIDE, BEHIND,
BELOW; 6. NEARBY; 7. UP,
DOWN, LEFT, RIGHT

DEFINITIONS 10

Fletcher: Maker of arrows;
Jussive: Expressing a command; **Demagogue:** Leader
of the populace; **Kibble:** To
grind coarsely; **Primogenitor:**
Earliest ancestor; **Sirdar:**
Person in command; **Whelm:**
Engulf, submerge; **Presage:**
Omen, portent; **Festal:** Of a
feast; **Apodal:** Without feet

COLUMN WORDS 10

S	H	A	N	D	Y
Y	E	L	L	O	W
P	A	N	I	C	S
A	L	L	O	T	S
S	T	U	P	O	R
C	H	E	E	R	S

STRINGS 10

There are many acceptable
answers. Example: DOCTOR,
RHUBARB, BREAKFAST,
TELEPHONE, EYE

COMBINED ANAGRAMS 10

TRUCK WAGON; AIRPLANE
TRAIN; HELICOPTER LINER;
BICYCLE SUBMARINE

QUOTE GRID 10

QUOTE: YOU HAVE TO
MAKE MORE NOISE THAN
ANYBODY ELSE, YOU
HAVE TO MAKE YOURSELF
MORE OBTRUSIVE THAN
ANYBODY ELSE, IF YOU
ARE REALLY GOING TO GET
YOUR REFORM REALIZED,
Emmeline Pankhurst
PHRASE: THE BRITISH
SUFFRAGETTE MOVEMENT

WORD CAPSULE 10

There are many acceptable
answers. Example: RECAP;
RANGE; RAYON; RELIC;
RADII; ROYAL IRATE; INDEX;
IONIC; IMAGE; IDEAL; INCUS

MISSING ALPHABET 10

The man was amazed at her
extreme reaction. "Darling, I'm
sorry" he said quietly "As it's
so important to you, I'd like to
offer to buy a taxi between us
and join the local Taxi Lovers'
Association."

MINI WORD SUDOKU 10

I	S	N	A	R	B
R	B	A	S	I	N
S	N	I	B	A	R
B	A	R	I	N	S
A	R	S	N	B	I
N	I	B	R	S	A

WORDS FROM A WORD 10

There are many acceptable
answers. Example:
Mercury
Otter, orang-utan
Beethoven, Brahms, Bach
Identify, invoking, immunity,
improved
Lesotho, Libya, Liberia,
Luxembourg, Laos
Egg, eggplant, enchilada,
endive, eel, elderberry

RHYMING WORDS 10

CUTE, DOUBT, MOAT, KITE,
STREET, SWEAT, WAIT
SQUASH, NIECE, CREPE

NAMES 10

Girl's name	Extra letter
PAULA	Z
ETHEL	S
SONYA	N
HOLLY	E
PATSY	U
EMILY / MILEY	N
ROSIE	A
SUZANNE	

REMEMBERING NAMES AND FACES 10

From top to bottom: Eduardo; Florence; Barry; Bernard; Rosa; Alexander; Grace; Cindy

CORRECTING SPELLING 10

Nothing seemed to embarrass Lizzy. She was fun, mischievous and laughed a lot. Attempts to discipline her at school failed, but teachers liked her nonetheless. Whenever she had some musical equipment she would break into song and turn every situation into a karaoke. While Lizzy was at the library her friends placed an enormous xylophone on her desk and waited with bated breath to see her reaction. Lizzy returned to her desk. Unperturbed, and with her usual abundance of enthusiasm, she picked up the mallets and showed herself to be a connoisseur of the instrument. The consensus of opinion was that Lizzy was an exceptionally gifted musician.

WORD SEARCH 10

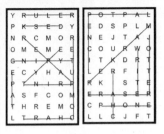

WORD LADDER 10

IFBE; IFBU; CFBU; CPBU; CPPU; GPPU Code: Take the following letter in the alphabet. HEAD, HEAT, BEAT, BOAT, BOOT, FOOT

CONTINUOUS WORDS 10

Amaze Eczema Amazing Gazebo Oozes Syzygy Wizardry Fizzy Frenzy Floozy Jazzy Razzmatazz Topaz Zany Buzzer Razor Ziggurat Waltz Zero Ozone Enzyme Frieze Frozen Zephyr Maize Muzzle Haze Glitzy Zaba- glione Craze Lizard Dazed Dozen Zinnia Pizza Plaza Zirconia Frizz Zesty Zigzag Gizmo Hertz Zoology Zebra Lazuli Squeeze Snoozed Geezer Zillion Zeppelin Chintz Zealous Schmaltz Zucchini Seize Zenith Sneezed Bronze Zodiac Zing Gazump Showbiz Zombie Vizier Kazoo Zooms Zoned Size Blitz Blaze Gazes Zippy

WEB WORDS 10

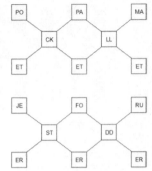

WORD CHAIN 10

There are many acceptable answers. Example:
EATING RATING RAVING SAVING SAYING LAYING LACING RACING FACING FARING CARING PARING
TASTES WASTES WASTER FASTER FATTER FITTER BITTER BATTER BUTTER CUTTER GUTTER MUTTER MATTER NATTER
FLYING FRYING CRYING DRYING TRYING PRYING PAYING LAYING LADING FADING WADING
PATTED PARTED PASTED POSTED POSTER FOSTER ROSTER ROTTER HOTTER JOTTER JOTTED JOLTED BOLTED
STRAWS STRAYS STRAPS STRIPS STRIPE STRIKE STROKE STRODE STRIDE STRIFE STRIVE

SOLVING SENTENCES 10

SOME WORDS ARE THE RIGHT WAY ROUND WHILE SOME ARE NOT AND FACE THE OTHER WAY.
(Words alternate between being written forwards and backwards, with incorrect breaks)

TWISTER 10

F	D	D	N	L
L	R	R	I	A
	O	A	A	M	
W	W	G	R
E	E	E	O	O
R	R	R	N	D

TEN ADJECTIVES 10

There are many acceptable answers. Example:
Xenophobic, xylophonic, xanthic, xylographic, xerographic, xerophilous, xiphoid, xenolithic , xerophthalmic, xerotic
Zippy, zesty, zany, zealous, zonked, zoological, zappy, zigzag, zodiacal, zoic

FIRST LETTER 10

New letters: PPOR
Word: PROP

PATTERNS 10

PATTERN: Words in the first column are made from letters with straight lines; words in the second column are made from letters that have curved lines; words in the third column are made with a mixture of the two.

LIZZY	COCO	RUTH
MATT	RUSS	JOHN
HILL	ROSCO	POOLE
MEAT	SOUP	BRAN
MINK	DOG	GORILLA
WAIL	PURR	GROAN

LETTER SQUARES 10

There are many acceptable answers. Example:
CHOLERA - ALCHEMY - YEARNED - DRASTIC DECISION - NEEDLESS - STARTING - GESTURED ATHLETICS - SAXOPHONE - EXCEEDING - GUERRILLA FORMIDABLE - EXPLOSIVES - SURRENDERS - SOUNDPROOF

FICTIONAL LANGUAGE 10

They arrived at the airport and checked in their BAGAQUI. Once aboard the EROPLAVI they were asked to fasten their KULINUPUX. Part way through watching the PELIKCIN, the food was served on their HALAHAX.

ANSWERS TO BONUS PUZZLES

TRIANGLES 1

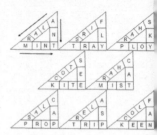

LETTER SHUFFLE 3

LIFE IS THE SCHOOL, LOVE IS THE LESSON

NINE WORDS 1

There are many acceptable answers. Example:
I AM THE BEST TEXAN PLAYER, WINNING CONTESTS REGULARLY